Happy Christm

All our love Maura + Feargus,

THE IRISH TIMES BOOK OF FAVOURITE IRISH POEMS

IRISH TIMES BOOKS

First published October 2000 by The Irish Times Limited
10 – 16 D'Olier Street, Dublin 2, Ireland.

Distribution: Irish Times Books
Telephone (01) 6792022 ext.8271
Fax (01) 6718446
email itbooks@irish-times.ie

10 9 8 7 6 5 4 3 2 1

ISBN 0 907011 31 4

Project Director: Brenda McNiff
Administration: Julie Dobson

Cover design: Terry Foley
Printed and Typeset in the Republic of Ireland
by Mahons Printers, Dublin.

CONTENTS

INTRODUCTION

I have a memory of a misty day on the strand in Curracloe. It must be the early 1960s. A neighbour is there with her husband and he is from Clare. My mother is there and my auntie Maeve. Maybe my father, and certainly two or three others. The adults are sitting on rugs and the children are swimming or playing in the sand. We are not meant to be listening to the adult conversation and if we are noticed doing so we are sent away. It is one of those days when everyone is poised to make a run for it if the mist hardens into rain. We watch the adults watching the clouds.

I don't much like the sea, or the sand, or the other children but I know that if I sit even on the edge of a rug and draw the slightest attention to myself one of the adults will tell me to go away and play. Nonetheless, I love listening to them and therefore approaching the adult rug stealthily is always worth trying.

My auntie Maeve is reciting poetry. She is sitting up and staring out to sea and her voice has the same stilted, serious and incantatory tone she uses when she is giving out the Rosary. All of the others have grown serious, each in different poses, one lying back, one resting on an elbow, one sitting up. My auntie Maeve has tears in her eyes. The poem is long and it rhymes. I wish I could remember what it was.

No one talks when she is finished. I know never to talk when the adults leave silence, because the next thing said is often the most unusual and unexpected. The next thing now is my mother. She is reciting The Lake Isle of Innisfree. I have heard her doing this before. Her voice is much softer and more dramatic than her Rosary-voice, but, like auntie Maeve, she does not take her eyes from the far distance when she recites. And something else too: for both of them reciting these poems evokes a terrible sadness which is far from the light, funny talk they normally have on the strand.

And then Pat Sheehan starts. He is a captain in the army and they have rented a house just beside the Winning Post. He is from Clare so his accent is different. He knows poems that they all seem to know, but they allow him recite them and join in only at the end of verses. He too stares out to sea when he recites. He recites the words slowly and carefully.

Then, the poetry fades, or my memory of it fades, and the scene melts back to ordinary talk. I don't know how long this lasts, but it is broken by my auntie Maeve, who in mid-talk without warning has started to recite another poem. The others all stop and pay attention, but she doesn't seem to mind about the others; she is reciting the poem to herself or to the sea or to some other power and all of the others recogise this and pay special attention. Once more she has tears in her eyes and I cannot stop looking at her.

My mother had two great mentors: a Mercy nun called Sister Catherine who taught her English until she left school to go to work at fourteen, and Anew MacMaster, whose troupe came to Enniscorthy when my mother was young and performed Shakespeare in a way that she never forgot. So for the rest of that holiday in Curracloe, once she discovered that Pat Sheehan liked poetry too, she could not stop reciting speeches from Othello or Julius Caesar as though she was Anew MacMaster on the stage of the Atheneum in Enniscorthy. At other times all through her later life, for no reason, she would begin to describe something Sister Catherine had said and then start reciting again from Shakespeare, Shelley, Tennyson, Keats or Yeats.

When she died, I found all her notebooks beside her bed, the first one dated 1941 when she was twenty, with poems written out in that beautiful hand-writing that Irish women of her generation had learned from nuns. She kept it up to the end of her life. The last notebook had poems by Sean Dunne, Michael Coady, Paul Durcan, Derek Mahon, Nuala Ni Dhomnnaill, Anthony Cronin, Seamus Heaney, Pat Boran and others cut out from the newspaper or written out in longhand. At her funeral, one of her school-friends began to talk about what a great teacher Sister Catherine was. Sixty-five years later, her old English teacher's presence was as vivid to her as it had been to my mother.

So much Irish writing begins in song as does so much Irish life. Joyce's work is full of song. He had a beautiful tenor voice. Beckett loved the Schubert lieder. And the Irish theatre in the twentieth century is full of song, from Yeats's plays to the plays of O'Casey, and later the plays of writers like Brian Friel, Tom Murphy, Sebastian Barry, Billy Roche. You feel that much Irish writing for the theatre, or even for the page, is a rich substitute for singing. And beside song there is prayer, the formal language of incantation and supplication. Irish poetry over the last hundred years has maintained its roots in song and prayer; it has, unlike poetry elsewhere, kept faith with its audience, it has been written for readers, to be cut out from the newspaper or copied out by hand, to be kept beside the bed, close to the prayer-book and the list of important telephone numbers. To be learned off by heart and recited in such a way that anyone listening, child or adult, could never forget the voice, the tone, the moment when the line ended and the rhyme hit home, and the strange, awed silence when the voice stopped reciting.

In Ireland in the twentieth century the best and the brightest became teachers. A career in teaching was considered then like becoming a computer millionaire is now, a natural choice of profession for someone with brains. For my mother and her school friends Sister Catherine offered them a sort of lasting inspiration. In the late 1960s much of the school curriculum changed in the Republic of Ireland and a new set of poems and poets were added to the masterpieces of Shakespare and Keats and Shelley and Yeats. It is remarkable how many of the poems chosen here are poems that were, or still are, part of the school curriculum. Thus poets like Patrick Kavanagh, Austin Clarke, F.R. Higgins and Thomas Kinsella entered the national imagination. Of the non-Irish poets in the new curriculum, perhaps the one who puzzled and intrigued most was T.S. Eliot. In St Peter's College in Wexford, in Father Larkin's class, we studied The Love Song of J. Alfred Prufrock. Most of us were from rural Ireland, many from farms; most had more interest in the GAA than T.S. Eliot; but everyone wanted to, or needed to, get the Leaving Certificate. And it was now clear that learning poems by rote would not help you, you had to understand the poems and know how to interpret them, make arguments about them. Father Larkin took us through the poem line by line. For most of us, this was a new sort of poem. None of us associated "a patient etherized upon a table" as a subject for poetry, and none of us had come across this veiled irony and knowing modernity before.

Slowly, the entire class became fascinated by the poem, and we must have studied it in class after class. What was "the overwhelming question", Father Larkin asked us, which the narrator was leading her to? Could it be named? One of the reasons why these poems learned in classrooms stay in the mind and in the affections is the way we were forced to concentrate on them like no one has ever forced us to concentrate on poems since. Father Larkin asked us to write out the possible words that such an overwhelming question might possibly be framed in. He made it clear that there was no right answer. And this is another reason why the study of poetry remains so powerful: there is no right answer.

We all wrote out our version of the question. And the next week Father Larkin came into the classrooms with our copybooks. Only one of us had come near, he said. Only one of us had understood what such a question might imply. I remember that the winning student had used the word "existential" and our teacher asked him to prepare a paper on existentialism for the following week. None of us in that class, as far as I know, went on to study philosophy and I was the only one, I think, who went on to study poetry. It was the only time in our lives, then, when we would pay attention to the language of philosophy and, for the rest of them, it was one of the only times they would attend to the language of a modern poem. For all of us, and clearly as this list of favourite Irish poems shows, for students of poetry in secondary schools all over Ireland, these classes were memorable and the poems learned then stayed in the mind.

Recently, I have been going through the photographs that my mother kept beside her bed close to the poems and the missal and the list of important telephone numbers. So many of them were taken on those beaches on the Wexford coast, black and white photographs of moments when she and her sister and their friends were young or when their children were young. It seems unbelievable that almost all of the adults who sat on that rug that day in Curracloe are dead. They were all as happy that summer, let us suppose, as they ever would be. They were on holidays. At night they went to the bar of the Strand Hotel; during the day they lay on the beach and swam and watched the sky in case the sun might come out once more. The women wore slacks. There was a lot of laughter. They had all known each other for years. And yet, at times, something else came to them, something brought them close to the strangeness and the mystery of things, away from their jokes and their stories and their easy talk and their holiday mood. At times poetry came to them. It came easily and naturally, but when it took over, it was not ordinary. It changed everything, like a new element, or a small opening in the sky. Everything about them then, how they spoke and listened, how they looked out at the grey-blue sea, seemed ready to make the most of the gift of poetry, take it on board, use it and remember it, allow it to offer a swell of resonance and meaning to the moment.

Colm Tóibín
October 2000.

Foreword

On the last day of the last century, *The Irish Times* published a list of the 100 Favourite Irish Poems of all time, on the initiative of Poetry Ireland/Éigse Éireann. Readers of the newspaper, more than 3,500 of them, had written or e-mailed giving their choices in both languages. All but two of the most nominated poems (for which copyright permission was unforthcoming) are published here.

We thought it would be instructive, to ask people what poems they actually kept by heart. We thought it would be a useful corrective to the emphasis we would naturally place here in Poetry Ireland, on living poets and their poetry. We also thought, perhaps more tenuously, that the range of suggested poems might give us a kind of X-ray of the national mind, or at least of that portion of the population which responded to our invitation.

The results of this open invitation were both surprising and unsurprising. We got a great deal of Yeats, and Heaney, and Kavanagh, as we'd expected. Austin Clarke made a brave showing, as did Louis MacNeice, but Anon let us down, only one appearance, and our contemporary poets in Irish are by and large absent. Perhaps the oddest thing, from our point of view, is how few poems by women were nominated. Almost as telling was the fact that so few of the most nominated poems were by living poets, with the expected exceptions of Eavan Boland, Paul Durcan and Paul Muldoon.

What to make of all this? First, and obviously, people's favourite poems tend to be poems they learned in their youth, almost always in school and by rote. Second, it seems to take a long time for poems to lodge in anything like the permanent memory: most of the nominated poems will be familiar to most of us, which suggests a kind of sifting process, time winnowing the chaff from the grain until only "the best" is left. I'm not entirely sure, though, that this is the case, since, to raise only one objection, there is a cumulative and self-reinforcing energy at work if what is good, being accepted as good, gives us the narrow framework in which we judge what is subsequently good. Third, the list as published here is necessarily of the poems people nominated. When we cross-checked to find the most nominated *poets*, as opposed to poems, we discovered that of the ten most nominated, seven are living. I am inclined to read this as evidence of the growth of a more selective memory, the individual making specific choices from favourite authors of what to guard and commit to memory, rather than accepting choices presented to them by teachers or other mediators.

The readers will understand that for reasons of space we publish here excerpts from a number of longer poems. As with the other poems in this anthology, we hope that these excerpts will send the reader to the poems and poets involved.

All of which said, like other anthologies this one should be read, first and foremost for the pleasure of what it contains. Here are good poems that have proved their ability to endure in time, to speak across generations and across the gulf of silence that necessarily isolates us from each other. Here are testaments to the endearing and enduring human signature, artifice blended with speech from the heart.

Theo Dorgan
Director
Poetry Ireland/Éigse Éireann
October, 2000.

FOREWORD

When I took over as Literary Editor of *The Irish Times* one of the happiest surprises of the job was the river of poetry that flows onto the desk every week: a "... gift /Utterly unasked for ..." as Sylvia Plath might have put it. In an at-times frenzied world of deadlines and decisions, of humming fax machines and never ending emails the regular, but unannounced, arrival of something as intimate as a poem remains a daily source of wonder. Yes, many of them are poor, but many are not. Also there is a levelling process at work here because while some come, without notice, from the big guns of contemporary Irish writing, others bear unknown names and there is a generosity going with both. They want to share their new poem with the world.

One look at the acknowledgements in myriad Irish anthologies will show how established is the tradition of publishing poems in *The Irish Times.* The fact that not just this newspaper, but also Irish newspapers in general, publish so much creative writing as a matter of course, is often remarked on as unique at international newspaper conferences. Sometimes, consciously but also unconsciously, the poems are linked to the newspaper's life's blood: News - as when my predecessor as Literary Editor John Banville published "Ceasefire" by Michael Longley in the paper coinciding with the announcement by the IRA of the first Northern Ireland ceasefire. The poem's first "electrifying appearance" in the newspaper had, said Nuala Ní Dhomhnaill, a galvanising effect that could only be imagined, of some lines perhaps, of Yeats, at the turn of a previous century.

Similarly as we pondered within the newspaper how to adequately mark the last Winter Solstice of the millennium at Newgrange, what appeared one December morning on the fax but "A Dream of Solstice" from Seamus Heaney: Dante translated, and then Meath-ified. It was on Page One a day or two later.

When Poetry Ireland proposed that we collectively ask people to nominate their favourite Irish poems of all time in either Irish or English, we knew it was the perfect way to engage the newspaper's readers in the closing, not just of a century, but of a millennium. As colleague and poet Katie Donovan put it when exhorting people to send in nominations, there was no shortage of sources. Had we not, she said, "voices more numerous and rich than any other nation of our size can claim".

The entries poured in and on the last day of 1999 the poems and poets most loved by readers of *The Irish Times* were celebrated in the paper. A memorable meeting also took place in Fleet Street at which Theo Dorgan and the newspaper's *General Services Manager* Brenda McNiff, who has so painstakingly put this book together, lilted their way through the Irish poetic canon in both languages, and the idea of putting the project between covers took flight. Now here it is.

Caroline Walsh
Literary Editor.
October, 2000.

The Lake Isle of Innisfree

I will arise and go now, and go to Innisfree,
And a small cabin build there, of clay and wattles made:
Nine bean-rows will I have there, a hive for the honey-bee,
And live alone in the bee-loud glade.

And I shall have some peace there, for peace comes dropping slow,
Dropping from the veils of the morning to where the cricket sings;
There midnight's all a glimmer, and noon a purple glow,
And evening full of the linnet's wings.

I will arise and go now, for always night and day
I hear lake water lapping with low sounds by the shore;
While I stand on the roadway, or on the pavements grey,
I hear it in the deep heart's core.

He Wishes for the Cloths of Heaven

Had I the heavens' embroidered cloths,
Enwrought with golden and silver light,
The blue and the dim and the dark cloths
Of night and light and the half-light,
I would spread the cloths under your feet:
But I, being poor, have only my dreams;
I have spread my dreams under your feet;
Tread softly because you tread on my dreams.

Mid-Term Break

I sat all morning in the college sick bay
Counting bells knelling classes to a close.
At two o'clock our neighbours drove me home.

In the porch I met my father crying —
He had always taken funerals in his stride —
And Big Jim Evans saying it was a hard blow.

The baby cooed and laughed and rocked the pram
When I came in, and I was embarrassed
By old men standing up to shake my hand

And tell me they were 'sorry for my trouble'.
Whispers informed strangers I was the eldest,
Away at school, as my mother held my hand

In hers and coughed out angry tearless sighs.
At ten o'clock the ambulance arrived
With the corpse, stanched and bandaged by the nurses.

Next morning I went up into the room. Snowdrops
And candles soothed the bedside; I saw him
For the first time in six weeks. Paler now,

Wearing a poppy bruise on his left temple,
He lay in the four-foot box as in his cot.
No gaudy scars, the bumper knocked him clear.

A four-foot box, a foot for every year.

The Song of Wandering Aengus

I went out to the hazel wood,
Because a fire was in my head,
And cut and peeled a hazel wand,
And hooked a berry to a thread;
And when white moths were on the wing,
And moth-like stars were flickering out,
I dropped the berry in a stream
And caught a little silver trout.

When I had laid it on the floor
I went to blow the fire aflame,
But something rustled on the floor,
And some one called me by my name:
It had become a glimmering girl
With apple blossom in her hair
Who called me by my name and ran
And faded through the brightening air.

Though I am old with wandering
Through hollow lands and hilly lands,
I will find out where she has gone,
And kiss her lips and take her hands;
And walk among long dappled grass,
And pluck till time and times are done
The silver apples of the moon,
The golden apples of the sun.

On Raglan Road

On Raglan Road on an autumn day I met her first and knew
That her dark hair would weave a snare that I might one day rue;
I saw the danger, yet I walked along the enchanted way,
And I said, let grief be a fallen leaf at the dawning of the day.

On Grafton Street in November we tripped lightly along the ledge
Of the deep ravine where can be seen the worth of passion's
pledge,
The Queen of Hearts still making tarts and I not making hay—
O I loved too much and by such by such is happiness thrown
away.

I gave her gifts of the mind I gave her the secret sign that's known
To the artists who have known the true gods of sound and stone
And word and tint. I did not stint for I gave her poems to say.
With her own name there and her own dark hair like clouds over
fields of May.

On a quiet street where old ghosts meet I see her walking now
Away from me so hurriedly my reason must allow
That I had wooed not as I should a creature made of clay—
When the angel wooes the clay he'd lose his wings at the dawn of
day.

Easter 1916

I have met them at close of day
Coming with vivid faces
From counter or desk among grey
Eighteenth-century houses.
I have passed with a nod of the head
Or polite meaningless words,
Or have lingered awhile and said
Polite meaningless words,
And thought before I had done
Of a mocking tale or a gibe
To please a companion
Around the fire at the club,
Being certain that they and I
But lived where motley is worn:
All changed, changed utterly:
A terrible beauty is born.

That woman's days were spent
In ignorant good-will,
Her nights in argument
Until her voice grew shrill.
What voice more sweet than hers
When, young and beautiful,
She rode to harriers?
This man had kept a school
And rode our wingèd horse;
This other his helper and friend
Was coming into his force;
He might have won fame in the end,
So sensitive his nature seemed,
So daring and sweet his thought.
This other man I had dreamed
A drunken, vainglorious lout.
He had done most bitter wrong
To some who are near my heart,
Yet I number him in the song;
He, too, has resigned his part
In the casual comedy;

He, too, has been changed in his turn,
Transformed utterly:
A terrible beauty is born.

Hearts with one purpose alone
Through summer and winter seem
Enchanted to a stone
To trouble the living stream.
The horse that comes from the road,
The rider, the birds that range
From cloud to tumbling cloud,
Minute by minute they change;
A shadow of cloud on the stream
Changes minute by minute;
A horse-hoof slides on the brim,
And a horse plashes within it;
The long-legged moor-hens dive,
And hens to moor-cocks call;
Minute by minute they live:
The stone's in the midst of all.

Too long a sacrifice
Can make a stone of the heart.
O when may it suffice?
That is Heaven's part, our part
To murmur name upon name,
As a mother names her child
When sleep at last has come
On limbs that had run wild.
What is it but nightfall?
No, no, not night but death;
Was it needless death after all?
For England may keep faith
For all that is done and said.
We know their dream; enough
To know they dreamed and are dead;
And what if excess of love
Bewildered them till they died?

I write it out in a verse —
MacDonagh and MacBride
And Connolly and Pearse
Now and in time to be,
Wherever green is worn,
Are changed, changed utterly:
A terrible beauty is born.

September 25 1916

When You are Old

When you are old and grey and full of sleep,
And nodding by the fire, take down this book,
And slowly read, and dream of the soft look
Your eyes had once, and of their shadows deep;

How many loved your moments of glad grace,
And loved your beauty with love false or true,
But one man loved the pilgrim soul in you,
And loved the sorrows of your changing face;

And bending down beside the glowing bars,
Murmur, a little sadly, how Love fled
And paced upon the mountains overhead
And hid his face amid a crowd of stars.

Canal Bank Walk

Leafy-with-love banks and the green waters of the canal
Pouring redemption for me, that I do
The will of God, wallow in the habitual, the banal,
Grow with nature again as before I grew.
The bright stick trapped, the breeze adding a third
Party to the couple kissing on an old seat,
And a bird gathering materials for the nest for the Word
Eloquently new and abandoned to its delirious beat.
O unworn world enrapture me, enrapture me in a web
Of fabulous grass and eternal voices by a beech,
Feed the gaping need of my senses, give me ad lib
To pray unselfconsciously with overflowing speech
For this soul needs to be honoured with a new dress woven
From green and blue things and arguments that cannot be proven.

STONY GREY SOIL

O stony grey soil of Monaghan
The laugh from my love you thieved;
You took the gay child of my passion
And gave me your clod-conceived.

You clogged the feet of my boyhood
And I believed that my stumble
Had the poise and stride of Apollo
And his voice my thick-tongued mumble.

You told me the plough was immortal!
O green-life-conquering plough!
Your mandril strained, your coulter blunted
In the smooth lea-field of my brow.

You sang on steaming dunghills
A song of cowards' brood,
You perfumed my clothes with weasel itch,
You fed me on swinish food.

You flung a ditch on my vision
Of beauty, love and truth.
O stony grey soil of Monaghan
You burgled my bank of youth!

Lost the long hours of pleasure
All the women that love young men.
O can I still stroke the monster's back
Or write with unpoisoned pen

His name in these lonely verses
Or mention the dark fields where
The first gay flight of my lyric
Got caught in a peasant's prayer.

Mullahinsha, Drummeril, Black Shanco —
Wherever I turn I see
In the stony grey soil of Monaghan
Dead loves that were born for me.

The Stolen Child

Where dips the rocky highland
Of Sleuth Wood in the lake,
There lies a leafy island
Where flapping herons wake
The drowsy water-rats;
There we've hid our faery vats,
Full of berries
And of reddest stolen cherries.
Come away, O human child!
To the waters and the wild
With a faery, hand in hand,
For the world's more full of weeping than you can understand.

Where the wave of moonlight glosses
The dim grey sands with light,
Far off by furthest Rosses
We foot it all the night,
Weaving olden dances,
Mingling hands and mingling glances
Till the moon has taken flight;
To and fro we leap
And chase the frothy bubbles,
While the world is full of troubles
And is anxious in its sleep.
Come away, O human child!
To the waters and the wild
With a faery, hand in hand,
For the world's more full of weeping than you can understand.

Where the wandering water gushes
From the hills above Glen-Car,
In pools among the rushes
That scarce could bathe a star,
We seek for slumbering trout
And whispering in their ears
Give them unquiet dreams;
Leaning softly out
From ferns that drop their tears

Over the young streams.
Come away, O human child!
To the waters and the wild
With a faery, hand in hand,
For the world's more full of weeping than you can understand.

Away with us he's going,
The solemn-eyed:
He'll hear no more the lowing
Of the calves on the warm hillside
Or the kettle on the hob
Sing peace into his breast,
Or see the brown mice bob
Round and round the oatmeal-chest.
For he comes, the human child,
To the waters and the wild
With a faery, hand in hand,
From a world more full of weeping than he can understand.

An Old Woman of the Roads

Oh, to have a little house!
To own the hearth and stool and all!
The heaped-up sods upon the fire,
The pile of turf against the wall!

To have a clock with weights and chains
And pendulum swinging up and down,
A dresser filled with shining delph,
Speckled and white and blue and brown!

I could be busy all the day
Clearing and sweeping hearth and floor,
And fixing on their shelf again
My white and blue and speckled store!

I could be quiet there at night
Beside the fire and by myself,
Sure of a bed and loth to leave
The ticking clock and the shining delph!

Och! but I'm weary of mist and dark,
And roads where there's never a house nor bush,
And tired I am of bog and road,
And the crying wind and the lonesome hush!

And I am praying to God on high,
And I am praying him night and day,
For a little house, a house of my own—
Out of the wind's and the rain's way.

IN MEMORY OF MY MOTHER

I do not think of you lying in the wet clay
Of a Monaghan graveyard; I see
You walking down a lane among the poplars
On your way to the station, or happily

Going to second Mass on a summer Sunday —
You meet me and you say:
'Don't forget to see about the cattle —'
Among your earthiest words the angels stray.

And I think of you walking along a headland
Of green oats in June,
So full of repose, so rich with life —
And I see us meeting at the end of a town

On a fair day by accident, after
The bargains are all made and we can walk
Together through the shops and stalls and markets
Free in the oriental streets of thought.

O you are not lying in the wet clay,
For it is a harvest evening now and we
Are piling up the ricks against the moonlight
And you smile up at us — eternally.

Sailing to Byzantium

I

That is no country for old men. The young
In one another's arms, birds in the trees
— Those dying generations - at their song,
The salmon-falls, the mackerel-crowded seas,
Fish, flesh, or fowl, commend all summer long
Whatever is begotten, born, and dies.
Caught in that sensual music all neglect
Monuments of unageing intellect.

II

An aged man is but a paltry thing,
A tattered coat upon a stick, unless
Soul clap its hands and sing, and louder sing
For every tatter in its mortal dress,
Nor is there singing school but studying
Monuments of its own magnificence;
And therefore I have sailed the seas and come
To the holy city of Byzantium.

III

O sages standing in God's holy fire
As in the gold mosaic of a wall,
Come from the holy fire, perne in a gyre,
And be the singing-masters of my soul.
Consume my heart away; sick with desire
And fastened to a dying animal
It knows not what it is; and gather me
Into the artifice of eternity.

IV

Once out of nature I shall never take
My bodily form from any natural thing,
But such a form as Grecian goldsmiths make
Of hammered gold and gold enamelling
To keep a drowsy Emperor awake;
Or set upon a golden bough to sing
To lords and ladies of Byzantium
Of what is past, or passing, or to come.

The Wild Swans at Coole

The trees are in their autumn beauty,
The woodland paths are dry,
Under the October twilight the water
Mirrors a still sky;
Upon the brimming water among the stones
Are nine-and-fifty swans.

The nineteenth autumn has come upon me
Since I first made my count;
I saw, before I had well finished,
All suddenly mount
And scatter wheeling in great broken rings
Upon their clamorous wings.

I have looked upon those brilliant creatures,
And now my heart is sore.
All's changed since I, hearing at twilight,
The first time on this shore,
The bell-beat of their wings above my head,
Trod with a lighter tread.

Unwearied still, lover by lover,
They paddle in the cold
Companionable streams or climb the air;
Their hearts have not grown old;
Passion or conquest, wander where they will,
Attend upon them still.

But now they drift on the still water,
Mysterious, beautiful;
Among what rushes will they build,
By what lake's edge or pool
Delight men's eyes when I awake some day
To find they have flown away?

from THE DESERTED VILLAGE

Sweet Auburn! loveliest village of the plain;
Where health and plenty cheered the labouring swain,
Where smiling spring its earliest visit paid,
And parting summer's lingering blooms delayed:
Dear lovely bowers of innocence and ease,
Seats of my youth, when every sport could please,
How often have I loitered o'er thy green,
Where humble happiness endeared each scene!
How often have I paused on every charm,
The sheltered cot, the cultivated farm,
The never-failing brook, the busy mill,
The decent church that topped the neighbouring hill,
The hawthorn bush, with seats beneath the shade,
For talking age and whispering lovers made! . . .

These were thy charms — but all these charms are fled.
Sweet smiling village, loveliest of the lawn,
Thy sports are fled, and all thy charms withdrawn:
Amidst thy bowers the tyrant's hand is seen,
And desolation saddens all thy green:
One only master grasps the whole domain,
And half a tillage stints thy smiling plain.
No more thy glassy brook reflects the day,
But, choked with sedges, works its weedy way;
Along thy glades, a solitary guest,
The hollow sounding bittern guards its nest;
Amidst thy desert walks the lapwing flies,
And tires their echoes with unvaried cries;
Sunk are thy bowers in shapeless ruin all,
And the long grass o'er-tops the mouldering wall;
And trembling, shrinking from the spoiler's hand,
Far, far away thy children leave the land.

Ill fares the land, to hastening ills a prey,
Where wealth accumulates, and men decay:
Princes and lords may flourish, or may fade;
A breath can make them, as a breath has made;
But a bold peasantry, their country's pride,
When once destroyed, can never be supplied. . . .

Beside yon straggling fence that skirts the way,
With blossomed furze unprofitably gay,
There, in his noisy mansion, skilled to rule,
The village master taught his little school.
A man severe he was, and stern to view;
Well had the boding tremblers learned to trace
The day's disasters in his morning face;
Full well they laughed with counterfeited glee
At all his jokes, for many a joke had he;
Full well the busy whisper circling round
Conveyed the dismal tidings when he frowned.
Yet he was kind, or, if severe in aught,
The love he bore to learning was in fault;
The village all declared how much he knew:
'Twas certain he could write, and cipher too;
Lands he could measure, terms and tides presage,
And even the story ran that he could gauge;
In arguing, too, the parson owned his skill,
For, even though vanquished, he could argue still;
While words of learned length and thundering sound
Amazed the gazing rustics ranged around;
And still they gazed, and still the wonder grew,
That one small head could carry all he knew. . . .

Even now the devastation is begun,
And half the business of destruction done;
Even now, methinks, as pondering here I stand,
I see the rural virtues leave the land.
Down where yon anchoring vessel spreads the sail
That idly waiting flaps with every gale,
Downward they move, a melancholy band,
Pass from the shore, and darken all the strand.
Contented toil, and hospitable care,
And kind connubial tenderness, are there;
And piety with wishes placed above,
And steady loyalty, and faithful love.
And thou, sweet Poetry, thou loveliest maid,
Still first to fly where sensual joys invade;
Unfit in these degenerate times of shame,
To catch the heart, or strike for honest fame;

Dear charming nymph, neglected and decried,
My shame in crowds, my solitary pride;
Thou source of all my bliss, and all my woe,
That found'st me poor at first, and keep'st me so;
Thou guide by which the nobler arts excel,
Thou nurse of every virtue fare thee well! . . .

from THE BALLAD OF READING GAOL

I

He did not wear his scarlet coat,
For blood and wine are red,
And blood and wine were on his hands
When they found him with the dead,
The poor dead woman whom he loved,
And murdered in her bed. . . .

II

I never saw a man who looked
With such a wistful eye
Upon that little tent of blue
Which prisoners call the sky,
And at every wandering cloud that trailed
Its ravelled fleeces by. . . .

III

We sewed the sacks, we broke the stones,
We turned the dusty drill:
We banged the tins, and bawled the hymns,
And sweated on the mill:
But in the heart of every man
Terror was lying still. . . .

At six o'clock we cleaned our cells,
At seven all was still,
But the sough and swing of a mighty wing
The prison seemed to fill,
For the Lord of Death with icy breath
Had entered in to kill. . . .

IV

There is no chapel on the day
On which they hang a man:
The Chaplain's heart is far too sick,
Or his face is far too wan,
Or there is that written in his eyes
Which none should look upon.

So they kept us close till nigh on noon,
And then they rang the bell,
And the warders with their jingling keys
Opened each listening cell,
And down the iron stair we tramped,
Each from his separate Hell.

Out into God's sweet air we went,
But not in wonted way,
For this man's face was white with fear,
And that man's face was grey,
And I never saw sad men who looked
So wistfully at the day.

I never saw sad men who looked
With such a wistful eye
Upon that little tent of blue
We prisoners called the sky,
And at every happy cloud that passed
In such strange freedom by. . . .

V

This too I know – and wise it were
If each could know the same –
That every prison that men build
Is built with bricks of shame,
And bound with bars lest Christ should see
How men their brothers maim. . . .

VI

In Reading gaol by Reading town
There is a pit of shame,
And in it lies a wretched man
Eaten by teeth of flame,
In a burning winding-sheet he lies,
And his grave has got no name.

And there, till Christ call forth the dead,
In silence let him lie:
No need to waste the foolish tear,

Or heave the windy sigh:
The man had killed the thing he loved,
And so he had to die.

And all men kill the thing they love,
By all let this be heard,
Some do it with a bitter look,
Some with a flattering word,
The coward does it with a kiss
The brave man with a sword!

September 1913

What need you, being come to sense,
But fumble in a greasy till
And add the halfpence to the pence
And prayer to shivering prayer, until
You have dried the marrow from the bone?
For men were born to pray and save:
Romantic Ireland's dead and gone,
It's with O'Leary in the grave.

Yet they were of a different kind,
The names that stilled your childish play,
They have gone about the world like wind,
But little time had they to pray
For whom the hangman's rope was spun,
And what, God help us, could they save?
Romantic Ireland's dead and gone,
It's with O'Leary in the grave.

Was it for this the wild geese spread
The grey wing upon every tide;
For this that all that blood was shed,
For this Edward Fitzgerald died,
And Robert Emmet and Wolfe Tone,
All that delirium of the brave?
Romantic Ireland's dead and gone,
It's with O'Leary in the grave.

Yet could we turn the years again,
And call those exiles as they were
In all their loneliness and pain,
You'd cry, 'Some woman's yellow hair
Has maddened every mother's son':
They weighed so lightly what they gave.
But let them be, they're dead and gone,
They're with O'Leary in the grave.

DIGGING

Between my finger and my thumb
The squat pen rests; snug as a gun.

Under my window, a clean rasping sound
When the spade sinks into gravelly ground:
My father, digging. I look down

Till his straining rump among the flowerbeds
Bends low, comes up twenty years away
Stooping in rhythm through potato drills
Where he was digging.

The coarse boot nestled on the lug, the shaft
Against the inside knee was levered firmly.
He rooted out tall tops, buried the bright edge deep
To scatter new potatoes that we picked,
Loving their cool hardness in our hands.

By God, the old man could handle a spade.
Just like his old man.

My grandfather cut more turf in a day
Than any other man on Toner's bog.
Once I carried him milk in a bottle
Corked sloppily with paper. He straightened up
To drink it, then fell to right away
Nicking and slicing neatly, heaving sods

Over his shoulder, going down and down
For the good turf. Digging.

The cold smell of potato mould, the squelch and slap
Of soggy peat, the curt cuts of an edge
Through living roots awaken in my head.
But I've no spade to follow men like them.

Between my fingers and my thumb
The squat pen rests.
I'll dig with it.

A Christmas Childhood

I

One side of the potato-pits was white with frost —
How wonderful that was, how wonderful!
And when we put our ears to the paling-post
The music that came out was magical.

The light between the ricks of hay and straw
Was a hole in Heaven's gable. An apple tree
With its December-glinting fruit we saw —
O you, Eve, were the world that tempted me

To eat the knowledge that grew in clay
And death the germ within it! Now and then
I can remember something of the gay
Garden that was childhood's. Again

The tracks of cattle to a drinking-place,
A green stone lying sideways in a ditch
Or any common sight the transfigured face
Of a beauty that the world did not touch.

II

My father played the melodeon
Outside at our gate;
There were stars in the morning east
And they danced to his music.

Across the wild bogs his melodeon called
To Lennons and Callans.
As I pulled on my trousers in a hurry
I knew some strange thing had happened.

Outside in the cow-house my mother
Made the music of milking;
The light of her stable-lamp was a star
And the frost of Bethlehem made it twinkle.

A water-hen screeched in the bog,
Mass-going feet
Crunched the wafer-ice on the pot-holes,
Somebody wistfully twisted the bellows wheel.

My child poet picked out the letters
On the grey stone,
In silver the wonder of a Christmas townland,
The winking glitter of a frosty dawn.

Cassiopeia was over
Cassidy's hanging hill,
I looked and three whin bushes rode across
The horizon — the Three Wise Kings.

An old man passing said:
'Can't he make it talk' —
The melodeon. I hid in the doorway
And tightened the belt of my box-pleated coat.

I nicked six nicks on the door-post
With my penknife's big blade —
There was a little one for cutting tobacco.
And I was six Christmases of age.

My father played the melodeon,
My mother milked the cows,
And I had a prayer like a white rose pinned
On the Virgin Mary's blouse.

The Wayfarer

The beauty of the world hath made me sad,
This beauty that will pass;
Sometimes my heart hath shaken with great joy
To see a leaping squirrel in a tree,
Or a red lady-bird upon a stalk,
Or little rabbits in a field at evening,
Lit by a slanting sun,
Or some green hill where shadows drifted by
Some quiet hill where mountainy man hath sown
And soon would reap; near to the gate of Heaven;
Or children with bare feet upon the sands
Of some ebbed sea, or playing on the streets
Of little towns in Connacht,
Things young and happy.
And then my heart hath told me:
These will pass,
Will pass and change, will die and be no more,
Things bright and green, things young and happy;
And I have gone upon my way
Sorrowful.

Advent

We have tested and tasted too much, lover —
Through a chink too wide there comes in no wonder.
But here in the Advent-darkened room
Where the dry black bread and the sugarless tea
Of penance will charm back the luxury
Of a child's soul, we'll return to Doom
The knowledge we stole but could not use.

And the newness that was in every stale thing
When we looked at it as children: the spirit-shocking
Wonder in a black slanting Ulster hill
Or the prophetic astonishment in the tedious talking
Of an old fool will awake for us and bring
You and me to the yard gate to watch the whins
And the bog-holes, cart-tracks, old stables where Time begins.

O after Christmas we'll have no need to go searching
For the difference that sets an old phrase burning —
We'll hear it in the whispered argument of a churning
Or in the streets where the village boys are lurching.
And we'll hear it among decent men too
Who barrow dung in gardens under trees,
Wherever life pours ordinary plenty.
Won't we be rich, my love and I, and please
God we shall not ask for reason's payment,
The why of heart-breaking strangeness in dreeping hedges
Nor analyse God's breath in common statement.
We have thrown into the dust-bin the clay-minted wages
Of pleasure, knowledge and the conscious hour —
And Christ comes with a January flower.

I See His Blood Upon The Rose

I see his blood upon the rose
And in the stars the glory of his eyes,
His body gleams amid eternal snows,
His tears fall from the skies.

I see his face in every flower;
The thunder and the singing of the birds
Are but his voice — and carven by his power
Rocks are his written words.

All pathways by his feet are worn,
His strong heart stirs the ever-beating sea,
His crown of thorns is twined with every thorn,
His cross is every tree.

from THE GREAT HUNGER

Clay is the word and clay is the flesh
Where the potato-gatherers like mechanised scarecrows move
Along the side-fall of the hill— Maguire and his men.
If we watch them an hour is there anything we can prove
Of life as it is broken-backed over the Book
Of Death? Here crows gabble over worms and frogs
And the gulls like old newspapers are blown clear of the hedges,
    luckily.
Is there some light of imagination in these wet clods?
Or why do we stand here shivering? . . .

Watch him, watch him, that man on a hill whose spirit
Is a wet sack flapping about the knees of time.
He lives that his little fields may stay fertile when his own body
Is spread in the bottom of a ditch under two coulters crossed in
    Christ's Name.

He was suspicious in his youth as a rat near strange bread,
When girls laughed; when they screamed he knew that meant
The cry of fillies in season. He could not walk
The easy road to destiny. He dreamt
The innocence of young brambles to hooked treachery.
O the grip, O the grip of irregular fields! No man escapes.
It could not be that back of the hills love was free
And ditches straight.
No monster hand lifted up children and put down apes
As here. . . .

Poor Paddy Maguire, a fourteen-hour day
He worked for years. It was he that lit the fire
And boiled the kettle and gave the cows their hay.
His mother tall hard as a Protestant spire
Came down the stairs barefoot at the kettle-call
And talked to her son sharply: 'Did you let
The hens out, you?' She had a venomous drawl
And a wizened face like moth-eaten leatherette. . . .

Once one day in June when he was walking
Among his cattle in the Yellow Meadow
He met a girl carrying a basket–
And he was then a young and heated fellow.
Too earnest, too earnest! He rushed beyond the thing
To the unreal. And he saw Sin
Written in letters larger than John Bunyan dreamt of.
For the strangled impulse there is no redemption. . . .

Sitting on a wooden gate,
Sitting on a wooden gate,
Sitting on a wooden gate
He didn't care a damn.
Said whatever came into his head,
Said whatever came into his head,
Said whatever came into his head
And inconsequently sang.
While his world withered away,
He had a cigarette to smoke and a pound to spend
On drink the next Saturday.
His cattle were fat
And his horses all that
Midsummer grass could make them. . . .

A year passed and another hurried after it
And Patrick Maguire was still six months behind life–
His mother six months ahead of it;
His sister straddle-legged across it:–
One leg in hell and the other in heaven
And between the purgatory of middle-aged virginity–
She prayed for release to heaven or hell.
His mother's voice grew thinner like a rust-worn knife
But it cut venomously as it thinned,
It cut him up in the middle till he became more woman than
    man,
And it cut through to his mind before the end. . . .

We may come out into the October reality, Imagination,
The sleety wind no longer slants to the black hill where Maguire
And his men are now collecting the scattered harness and baskets.

The dog sitting on a wisp of dry stalks
Watches them through the shadows.
'Back in, back in.' One talks to the horse as to a brother.
Maguire himself is patting a potato-pit against the weather –
An old man fondling a new-piled grave:
'Joe, I hope you didn't forget to hide the spade,
For there's rogues in the townland. Hide it flat in a furrow.
I think we ought to be finished by to-morrow.'
Their voices through the darkness sound like voices from a cave,
A dull thudding far away, futile, feeble, far away,
First cousins to the ghosts of the townland. . . .

He stands in the doorway of his house
A ragged sculpture of the wind,
October creaks the rotted mattress,
The bedposts fall. No hope. No lust.
The hungry fiend
Screams the apocalypse of clay
In every corner of this land.

Thomas McDonagh

He shall not hear the bittern cry
In the wild sky, where he is lain.
Nor voices of the sweeter birds
Above the wailing of the rain.

Nor shall he know when loud March blows
Thro' slanting snows her fanfare shrill.
Blowing to flame the golden cup
Of many an upset daffodil.

And when the Dark Cow leaves the moor,
And pastures poor with greedy weeds,
Perhaps he'll hear her low at morn
Lifting her horn in pleasant meads.

THE MOTHER

I do not grudge them: Lord, I do not grudge
My two strong sons that I have seen go out
To break their strength and die, they and a few,
In bloody protest for a glorious thing,
They shall be spoken of among their people,
The generations shall remember them,
And call them blessed;
But I will speak their names to my own heart
In the long nights;
The little names that were familiar once
Round my dead hearth.
Lord, thou art hard on mothers:
We suffer in their coming and their going;
And tho' I grudge them not, I weary, weary
Of the long sorrow — And yet I have my joy:
My sons were faithful, and they fought.

THE PLANTER'S DAUGHTER

When night stirred at sea
And the fire brought a crowd in,
They say that her beauty
Was music in mouth
And few in the candlelight
Thought her too proud,
For the house of the planter
Is known by the trees.

Men that had seen her
Drank deep and were silent,
The women were speaking
Wherever she went —
As a bell that is rung
Or a wonder told shyly,
And O she was the Sunday
In every week.

ó CAOINEADH AIRT UÍ LAOGHAIRE

B'fhéidir gur aithris Eibhlín na dréachtaí seo
os cionn an choirp i gCarraig an Ime.

Mo ghrá go daingean tu!
Lá dá bhfaca thu
ag ceann tí an mhargaidh,
thug mo shúil aire dhuit,
thug mo chroí taitneamh duit,
d'éalaíos óm charaid leat
i bhfad ó bhaile leat.

Is domhsa nárbh aithreach:
Chuiris parlús á ghealadh dhom,
rúmanna á mbreacadh dhom,
bácús á dheargadh dhom,
brící á gceapadh dhom,
rósta ar bhearaibh dom,
mairt á leagadh dhom;
codladh i gclúmh lachan dom
go dtíodh an t-eadartha
nó thairis dá dtaitneadh liom.

Mo chara go daingean tu!
is cuimhin lem aigne
an lá breá earraigh úd,
gur bhreá thíodh hata dhuit
faoi bhanda óir tarraingthe;
claíomh cinn airgid,
lámh dheas chalma,
rompsáil bhagarthach —

fír-chritheagla
ar haid chealgach —
tú i gcóir chun falaracht
is each caol ceannann fút.
D'umhlaídis Sasanaigh
síos go talamh duit,
is ní ar mhaithe leat

ach le haon-chorp eagla,
cé gur leo a cailleadh tu,
a mhuirnín mh'anama . . . .

Mo chara thú go daingean!
is níor chreideas riamh dod mharbh
gur tháinig chugham do chapall
is a srianta léi go talamh,
is fuil do chroí ar a leacain
siar go t'iallait ghreanta
mar a mbíotheá id shuí 's id sheasamh.
Thugas léim go tairsigh,
an dara léim go geata,
an tríú léim ar do chapall.

Translation Thomas Kinsella page 138.

Among School Children

I

I walk through the long schoolroom questioning;
A kind old nun in a white hood replies;
The children learn to cipher and to sing,
To study reading-books and histories,
To cut and sew, be neat in everything
In the best modern way - the children's eyes
In momentary wonder stare upon
A sixty-year-old smiling public man.

II

I dream of a Ledaean body, bent
Above a sinking fire, a tale that she
Told of a harsh reproof, or trivial event
That changed some childish day to tragedy —
Told, and it seemed that our two natures blent
Into a sphere from youthful sympathy,
Or else, to alter Plato's parable,
Into the yolk and white of the one shell.

III

And thinking of that fit of grief or rage
I look upon one child or t'other there
And wonder if she stood so at that age —
For even daughters of the swan can share
Something of every paddler's heritage —
And had that colour upon cheek or hair,
And thereupon my heart is driven wild:
She stands before me as a living child.

IV

Her present image floats into the mind —
Did Quattrocento finger fashion it
Hollow of cheek as though it drank the wind
And took a mess of shadows for its meat?
And I though never of Ledaean kind
Had pretty plumage once - enough of that,
Better to smile on all that smile, and show
There is a comfortable kind of old scarecrow.

V

What youthful mother, a shape upon her lap
Honey of generation had betrayed,
And that must sleep, shriek, struggle to escape
As recollection or the drug decide,
Would think her son, did she but see that shape
With sixty or more winters on its head,
A compensation for the pang of his birth,
Or the uncertainty of his setting forth?

VI

Plato thought nature but a spume that plays
Upon a ghostly paradigm of things;
Solider Aristotle played the taws
Upon the bottom of a king of kings;
World-famous golden-thighed Pythagoras
Fingered upon a fiddle-stick or strings
What a star sang and careless Muses heard:
Old clothes upon old sticks to scare a bird.

VII

Both nuns and mothers worship images,
But those the candles light are not as those
That animate a mother's reveries,
But keep a marble or a bronze repose.
And yet they too break hearts - O Presences
That passion, piety or affection knows,
And that all heavenly glory symbolise —
O self-born mockers of man's enterprise;

VIII

Labour is blossoming or dancing where
The body is not bruised to pleasure soul,
Nor beauty born out of its own despair,
Nor blear-eyed wisdom out of midnight oil.
O chestnut-tree, great-rooted blossomer,
Are you the leaf, the blossom or the bole?
O body swayed to music, O brightening glance,
How can we know the dancer from the dance?

The Second Coming

Turning and turning in the widening gyre
The falcon cannot hear the falconer;
Things fall apart; the centre cannot hold;
Mere anarchy is loosed upon the world,
The blood-dimmed tide is loosed, and everywhere
The ceremony of innocence is drowned;
The best lack all conviction, while the worst
Are full of passionate intensity.

Surely some revelation is at hand;
Surely the Second Coming is at hand.
The Second Coming! Hardly are those words out
When a vast image out of *Spiritus Mundi*
Troubles my sight: somewhere in sands of the desert
A shape with lion body and the head of a man,
A gaze blank and pitiless as the sun,
Is moving its slow thighs, while all about it
Reel shadows of the indignant desert birds.
The darkness drops again; but now I know
That twenty centuries of stony sleep
Were vexed to nightmare by a rocking cradle,
And what rough beast, its hour come round at last,
Slouches towards Bethlehem to be born?

Inniskeen Road: July Evening

The bicycles go by in twos and threes —
There's a dance in Billy Brennan's barn to-night,
And there's the half-talk code of mysteries
And the wink-and-elbow language of delight.
Half-past eight and there is not a spot
Upon a mile of road, no shadow thrown
That might turn out a man or woman, not
A footfall tapping secrecies of stone.

I have what every poet hates in spite
Of all the solemn talk of contemplation.
Oh, Alexander Selkirk knew the plight
Of being king and government and nation.
A road, a mile of kingdom, I am king
Of banks and stones and every blooming thing.

Lines written on a seat on the Grand Canal, Dublin, 'Erected to the Memory of Mrs Dermot O'Brien'

O commemorate me where there is water,
Canal water preferably, so stilly
Greeny at the heart of summer. Brother
Commemorate me thus beautifully.
Where by a lock Niagariously roars
The falls for those who sit in the tremendous silence
Of mid-July. No one will speak in prose
Who finds his way to these Parnassian islands.
A swan goes by head low with many apologies,
Fantastic light looks through the eyes of bridges —
And look! a barge comes bringing from Athy
And other far-flung towns mythologies.
O commemorate me with no hero-courageous
Tomb — just a canal-bank seat for the passer-by.

An Irish Airman Foresees His Death

I know that I shall meet my fate
Somewhere among the clouds above;
Those that I fight I do not hate,
Those that I guard I do not love;
My country is Kiltartan Cross,
My countrymen Kiltartan's poor,
No likely end could bring them loss
Or leave them happier than before.
Nor law, nor duty bade me fight,
Nor public men, nor cheering crowds,
A lonely impulse of delight
Drove to this tumult in the clouds;
I balanced all, brought all to mind,
The years to come seemed waste of breath,
A waste of breath the years behind
In balance with this life, this death.

from CLEARANCES

in memoriam M.K.H., 1911–1984

She taught me what her uncle once taught her:
How easily the biggest coal block split
If you got the grain and hammer angled right.

The sound of that relaxed alluring blow,
Its co-opted and obliterated echo,
Taught me to hit, taught me to loosen,

Taught me between the hammer and the block
To face the music. Teach me now to listen,
To strike it rich behind the linear black.

I

A cobble thrown a hundred years ago
Keeps coming at me, the first stone
Aimed at a great-grandmother's turncoat brow.
The pony jerks and the riot's on.
She's crouched low in the trap
Running the gauntlet that first Sunday
Down the brae to Mass at a panicked gallop.
He whips on through the town to cries of 'Lundy!'

Call her 'The Convert'. 'The Exogamous Bride'.
Anyhow, it is a genre piece
Inherited on my mother's side
And mine to dispose with now she's gone.
Instead of silver and Victorian lace,
The exonerating, exonerated stone.

III

When all the others were away at Mass
I was all hers as we peeled potatoes.
They broke the silence, let fall one by one
Like solder weeping off the soldering iron:
Cold comforts set between us, things to share
Gleaming in a bucket of clean water.
And again let fall. Little pleasant splashes
From each other's work would bring us to our senses.

So while the parish priest at her bedside
Went hammer and tongs at the prayers for the dying
And some were responding and some crying
I remembered her head bent towards my head,
Her breath in mine, our fluent dipping knives —
Never closer the whole rest of our lives.

V

The cool that came off sheets just off the line
Made me think the damp must still be in them
But when I took my corners of the linen
And pulled against her, first straight down the hem
And then diagonally, then flapped and shook
The fabric like a sail in a cross-wind,
They made a dried-out undulating thwack.
So we'd stretch and fold and end up hand to hand
For a split second as if nothing had happened
For nothing had that had not always happened
Beforehand, day by day, just touch and go,
Coming close again by holding back
In moves where I was X and she was O
Inscribed in sheets she'd sewn from ripped-out flour sacks. . . .

VIII

I thought of walking round and round a space
Utterly empty, utterly a source
Where the decked chestnut tree had lost its place
In our front hedge above the wallflowers.
The white chips jumped and jumped and skited high.
I heard the hatchet's differentiated
Accurate cut, the crack, the sigh
And collapse of what luxuriated
Through the shocked tips and wreckage of it all.
Deep-planted and long gone, my coeval
Chestnut from a jam jar in a hole,
Its heft and hush become a bright nowhere,
A soul ramifying and forever
Silent, beyond silence listened for.

Epic

I have lived in important places, times
When great events were decided, who owned
That half a rood of rock, a no-man's land
Surrounded by our pitchfork-armed claims.
I heard the Duffys shouting 'Damn your soul'
And old McCabe stripped to the waist, seen
Step the plot defying blue cast-steel —
'Here is the march along these iron stones'
That was the year of the Munich bother. Which
Was more important? I inclined
To lose my faith in Ballyrush and Gortin
Till Homer's ghost came whispering to my mind
He said: I made the Iliad from such
A local row. Gods make their own importance.

ANOTHER SEPTEMBER

Dreams fled away, this country bedroom, raw
With the touch of the dawn, wrapped in a minor peace,
Hears through an open window the garden draw
Long pitch black breaths, lay bare its apple trees,
Ripe pear trees, brambles, windfall-sweetened soil,
Exhale rough sweetness against the starry slates.
Nearer the river sleeps St. John's, all toil
Locked fast inside a dream with iron gates.

Domestic Autumn, like an animal
Long used to handling by those countrymen,
Rubs her kind hide against the bedroom wall
Sensing a fragrant child come back again
— Not this half-tolerated consciousness,
Its own cold season never done,
But that unspeaking daughter, growing less
Familiar where we fell asleep as one.

Wakeful moth-wings blunder near a chair,
Toss their light shell at the glass, and go
To inhabit the living starlight. Stranded hair
Stirs on the still linen. It is as though
The black breathing that billows her sleep, her name,
Drugged under judgment, waned and—bearing daggers
And balances—down the lampless darkness they came,
Moving like women: Justice, Truth, such figures.

The Lost Heifer

When the black herds of the rain were grazing
In the gap of the pure cold wind
And the watery hazes of the hazel
Brought her into my mind,
I thought of the last honey by the water
That no hive can find.

Brightness was drenching through the branches
When she wandered again,
Turning the silver out of dark grasses
Where the skylark had lain,
And her voice coming softly over the meadow
Was the mist becoming rain.

JUNE

Broom out the floor now, lay the fender by,
And plant this bee-sucked bough of woodbine there,
And let the window down. The butterfly
Floats in upon the sunbeam, and the fair
Tanned face of June, the nomad gipsy, laughs
Above her widespread wares, the while she tells
The farmers' fortunes in the fields, and quaffs
The water from the spider-peopled wells.

The hedges are all drowned in green grass seas,
And bobbing poppies flare like Elmo's light,
While siren-like the pollen-stained bees
Drone in the clover depths. And up the height
The cuckoo's voice is hoarse and broke with joy.
And on the lowland crops the crows make raid,
Nor fear the clappers of the farmer's boy,
Who sleeps, like drunken Noah, in the shade.

And loop this red rose in that hazel ring
That snares your little ear, for June is short
And we must joy in it and dance and sing,
And from her bounty draw her rosy worth.
Ay! soon the swallows will be flying south,
The wind wheel north to gather in the snow,
Even the roses spilt on youth's red mouth
Will soon blow down the road all roses go.

SNOW

The room was suddenly rich and the great bay-window was
Spawning snow and pink roses against it
Soundlessly collateral and incompatible:
World is suddener than we fancy it.

World is crazier and more of it than we think,.
Incorrigibly plural. I peel and portion
A tangerine and spit the pips and feel
The drunkenness of things being various.

And the fire flames with a bubbling sound for world
Is more spiteful and gay than one supposes –
On the tongue on the eyes on the ears in the palms of one's
hands –
There is more than glass between the snow and the huge roses.

Personal Helicon

for Michael Longley

As a child, they could not keep me from wells
And old pumps with buckets and windlasses.
I loved the dark drop, the trapped sky, the smells
Of waterweed, fungus and dank moss.

One, in a brickyard, with a rotted board top.
I savoured the rich crash when a bucket
Plummeted down at the end of a rope.
So deep you saw no reflection in it.

A shallow one under a dry stone ditch
Fructified like any aquarium.
When you dragged out long roots from the soft mulch
A white face hovered over the bottom.

Others had echoes, gave back your own call
With a clean new music in it. And one
Was scaresome, for there, out of ferns and tall
Foxgloves, a rat slapped across my reflection.

Now, to pry into roots, to finger slime,
To stare, big-eyed Narcissus, into some spring
Is beneath all adult dignity. I rhyme
To see myself, to set the darkness echoing.

Raifteirí an File

Mise Raifteirí an file
Lán dóchais agus grá,
Le súile gan solas,
Le ciúnas gan chrá.

Ag dul siar ar m'aistear
Le solas mo chroí,
Fann agus tuirseach
Go deireadh mo shlí.

Féach anois mé
Agus m'aghaidh ar bhalla,
Ag seinm ceoil
Do phócaí folamh'.

Translation Criostóir Ó Floinn page 140.

MIRROR IN FEBRUARY

The day dawns with scent of must and rain,
Of opened soil, dark trees, dry bedroom air.
Under the fading lamp, half dressed — my brain
Idling on some compulsive fantasy —
I towel my shaven lip and stop, and stare,
Riveted by a dark exhausted eye,
A dry downturning mouth.

It seems again that it is time to learn,
In this untiring, crumbling place of growth
To which, for the time being, I return.
Now plainly in the mirror of my soul
I read that I have looked my last on youth
And little more; for they are not made whole
That reach the age of Christ.

Below my window the awakening trees,
Hacked clean for better bearing, stand defaced
Suffering their brute necessities,
And how should the flesh not quail that span for span
Is mutilated more? In slow distaste
I fold my towel with what grace I can,
Not young and not renewable, but man.

ó CÚIRT AN MHEÁN OÍCHE

'Míle fáilte is gáirdeas cléibh romhat,
A Aoibheall, a fháidhbhean ársa ón Léithchraig,
A shoilse an lae is a ré gan choimse,
A shaibhreas saolta i ngéibheann daoirse,
A cheannasach bhuach ó shluaite an aoibhnis,
Dob easnamh crua thú i dTuain 's i dTír Luirc.
Cúis mo cháis, is fáth mo chaointe,
Cúis do chráigh mé, is d'fhág mé cloíte,
Bhain dem threoir mé, is sheoil gan chiall mé,
Is chaith mar cheo mé dóite i bpianta:
Na sluaite imíonn gan chríoch, gan chaomhnadh,
Ar fuaid an tsaoil seo d'fhíorscoith béithe
'Na gcailleacha dubha gan chumhdach céile,
Caite gan chlú, gan chionta claonbhirt.
Is aithnid dom féin sa mhéid seo dem shiúlta
Bean agus céad nár mhéin leo a dhiúltadh
— Is mise 'na measc, mo chreach mar táimse! —
D'imigh 'na spaid gan fear gan pháiste.
Mo dhochar, mo dhódh, mo bhrón mar bhíom,
Gan sochar gan seoid gan só gan síth,
Go doilbhir duaibhseach duamhar dítheach,
Gan chodladh gan suan gan suairceas oíche,
Ach maslaithe i mbuairt, gan suaineas sínte,
Ar leabain leamhfhuar dár suathadh ag smaointe!

A cháidh na Craige! breathain go bíogach
Mná na Banba in anacra suíte,
Ar nós, má leanaid na fearaibh dá bhfuadar
Ó, mo lagar, ach caithfeamna a bhfuadach!
'Sé am ar mhéin leo céile a phósadh
An t-am nár mhéin le héinne góil leo,
An t-am nárbhil fhiú bheith fúthu sínte
— Seandaigh thamhanda shúite chloíte!
Dá dtiteadh amach le teas na hóige
Duine fén seacht ar theacht féasóige
Ceangal le mnaoi, ní míntais thoghfaidh,
Taithneamhach shuíte de shíol ná d'fhoghluim,
Clódheas chaoin ná míonla mhánla,
Arb eol di suí nó tíocht do láthair,
Ach doineantach odhar nó donn doilíosach
Chruinnigh le doghraing cabhair nár chuí dhi! . . .'

Translation David Marcus page 141.

Cill Chais

Cad a dhéanfaimid feasta gan adhmad?
Tá deireadh na gcoillte ar lár;
níl trácht ar Chill Chais ná ar a teaghlach
is ní chluinfear a cling go bráth.
An áit úd a gcónaíodh an deighbhean
fuair gradam is meidhir thar mhnáibh,
bhíodh iarlaí ag tarraingt tar toinn ann
is an t-aifreann binn á rá.

Ní chluinim fuaim lachan ná gé ann,
ná fiolar ag éamh cois cuain,
ná fiú na mbeacha chun saothair
thabharfadh mil agus céir don tslua.
Níl ceol binn milis na n-éan ann
le hamharc an lae a dhul uainn,
ná an chuaichín i mbarra na ngéag ann,
ós í chuirfeadh an saol chun suain.

Tá ceo ag titim ar chraobha ann
ná glanann le gréin ná lá,
tá smúid ag titim ón spéir ann
is a cuid uisce go léir ag trá.
Níl coll, níl cuileann, níl caor ann,
ach clocha is maolchlocháin,
páirc an chomhair gan chraobh ann
is d'imigh an géim chun fáin.

Anois mar bharr ar gach míghreann,
chuaigh prionsa na nGael thar sáil,
anonn le hainnir na míne
fuair gradam sa bhFrainc is sa Spáinn.

Anois tá a cuallacht á caoineadh,
gheibheadh airgead buí agus bán;
's í ná tógfadh seilbh na ndaoine,
ach cara na bhfíorbhochtán.

Aicim ar Mhuire is ar Íosa
go dtaga sí arís chughainn slán,
go mbeidh rincí fada ag gabháil timpeall,
ceol veidhlín is tinte cnámh;
go dtógtar an baile seo ár sinsear
Cill Chais bhreá arís go hard,
is go bráth nó go dtiocfaidh an díle
ná feictear é arís ar lár.

Translation Thomas Kinsella page 142.

The Fiddler of Dooney

When I play on my fiddle in Dooney,
Folk dance like a wave of the sea;
My cousin is priest in Kilvarnet,
My brother in Mocharabuiee.

I passed my brother and cousin:
They read in their books of prayer;
I read in my book of songs
I bought at the Sligo fair.

When we come at the end of time
To Peter sitting in state,
He will smile on the three old spirits,
But call me first through the gate;

For the good are always the merry,
Save by an evil chance,
And the merry love the fiddle,
And the merry love to dance:

And when the folk there spy me,
They will all come up to me,
With 'Here is the fiddler of Dooney!'
And dance like a wave of the sea.

THE BLACKBIRD OF DERRYCAIRN

Stop, stop and listen for the bough top
Is whistling and the sun is brighter
Than God's own shadow in the cup now!
Forget the hour-bell. Mournful matins
Will sound, Patric, as well at nightfall.

Faintly through mist of broken water
Fionn heard my melody in Norway.
He found the forest track, he brought back
This beak to gild the branch and tell, there,
Why men must welcome in the daylight.

He loved the breeze that warns the black grouse,
The shout of gillies in the morning
When packs are counted and the swans cloud
Loch Erne, but more than all those voices
My throat rejoicing from the hawthorn.

In little cells behind a cashel,
Patric, no handbell gives a glad sound.
But knowledge is found among the branches.
Listen! That song that shakes my feathers
Will thong the leather of your satchels.

Blackberry-Picking

for Philip Hobsbaun

Late August, given heavy rain and sun
For a full week, the blackberries would ripen.
At first, just one, a glossy purple clot
Among others, red, green, hard as a knot.
You ate that first one and its flesh was sweet
Like thickened wine: summer's blood was in it
Leaving stains upon the tongue and lust for
Picking. Then red ones inked up and that hunger
Sent us out with milk cans, pea tins, jam pots
Where briars scratched and wet grass bleached our boots.
Round hayfields, cornfields and potato drills
We trekked and picked until the cans were full,
Until the tinkling bottom had been covered
With green ones, and on top big dark blobs burned
Like a plate of eyes. Our hands were peppered
With thorn pricks, our palms sticky as Bluebeard's.

We hoarded the fresh berries in the byre
But when the bath was filled we found a fur,
A rat-grey fungus, glutting on our cache.
The juice was stinking too. Once off the bush
The fruit fermented, the sweet flesh would turn sour.
I always felt like crying. It wasn't fair
That all the lovely canfuls smelt of rot.
Each year I hoped they'd keep, knew they would not.

Spraying the Potatoes

The barrels of blue potato-spray
Stood on a headland of July
Beside an orchard wall where roses
Were young girls hanging from the sky.

The flocks of green potato-stalks
Were blossom spread for sudden flight,
The Kerr's Pinks in a frivelled blue,
The Arran Banners wearing white.

And over that potato-field
A lazy veil of woven sun.
Dandelions growing on headlands, showing
Their unloved hearts to everyone.

And I was there with the knapsack sprayer
On the barrel's edge poised. A wasp was floating
Dead on a sunken briar leaf
Over a copper-poisoned ocean.

The axle-roll of a rut-locked cart
Broke the burnt stick of noon in two.
An old man came through a cornfield
Remembering his youth and some Ruth he knew.

He turned my way. 'God further the work.'
He echoed an ancient farming prayer.
I thanked him. He eyed the potato-drills.
He said: 'You are bound to have good ones there.'

We talked and our talk was a theme of kings,
A theme for strings. He hunkered down
In the shade of the orchard wall. O roses
The old man dies in the young girl's frown.

And poet lost to potato-fields,
Remembering the lime and copper smell
Of the spraying barrels he is not lost
Or till blossomed stalks cannot weave a spell.

from A PINT OF PLAIN IS YOUR ONLY MAN
THE WORKMAN'S FRIEND,

The name or title of the pome I am about to recite, gentlemen, said Shanahan with leisure priest-like in character, is a pome by the name of the 'Workman's Friend'. By God you can't beat it. I've heard it praised by the highest. It's a pome about a thing that's known to all of us. It's about a drink of porter. . . .

When things go wrong and will not come right,
Though you do the best you can,
When life looks black as the hour of night —
A PINT OF PLAIN IS YOUR ONLY MAN.

When money's tight and is hard to get
And your horse has also ran,
When all you have is a heap of debt —
A PINT OF PLAIN IS YOUR ONLY MAN.

When health is bad and your heart feels strange,
And your face is pale and wan,
When doctors say that you need a change,
A PINT OF PLAIN IS YOUR ONLY MAN.

When food is scarce and your larder bare
And no rashers grease your pan,
When hunger grows as your meals are rare —
A PINT OF PLAIN IS YOUR ONLY MAN.

In time of trouble and lousy strife,
You have still got a darlint plan,
You still can turn to a brighter life —
A PINT OF PLAIN IS YOUR ONLY MAN. . . .

There's one thing in that pome, permanence, *if you know what I mean. That pome, I mean to say, is a pome that'll be heard wherever the Irish race is wont to gather, it'll live as long as there's a hard root of an Irishman left by the Almighty on this planet, mark my words.*

CONTAE MHAIGH EO
ANOIS TEACHT AN EARRAIGH

Anois teacht an earraigh, beidh an lá ag dul chun síneadh,
Is tar éis na Féil' Bríde ardóidh mé mo sheol,
Ó chuir mé im cheann é ní stopfaidh mé choíche
Go seasfa' mé thíos i lár Chontae Mhaigh Eo.
I gClár Clainne Mhuiris a bheas mé an chéad oíche,
'S i mBalla taobh thíos de 'thosós mé ag ól,
Go Coillte Mach rachad go ndéanfad cuairt mhíosa ann,
I bhfogas dhá mhíle do Bhéal an Áth' Mhóir.

Fágaim le huacht é go n-éiríonn mo chroíse
Mar éiríos an ghaoth nó mar 'scaipeas an ceo
Nuair a smaoiním ar Chearra nó ar Ghaileang taobh thíos de
Ar Sceathach a'Mhíle nó ar phlánaí Mhaigh Eo.
Cill Aodáin an baile a bhfásann gach ní ann,
Tá sméara 's sú craobh ann is meas ar gach sórt,
Is dá mbeinnse 'mo sheasamh i gceartlár mo dhaoine
D'imeodh an aois díom is bheinn arís óg.

Translation Críostóir Ó Floinn page 144.

The Circus Animals' Desertion

I

I sought a theme and sought for it in vain,
I sought it daily for six weeks or so.
Maybe at last, being but a broken man,
I must be satisfied with my heart, although
Winter and summer till old age began
My circus animals were all on show,
Those stilted boys, that burnished chariot,
Lion and woman and the Lord knows what.

II

What can I but enumerate old themes?
First that sea-rider Oisin led by the nose
Through three enchanted islands, allegorical dreams,
Vain gaiety, vain battle, vain repose,
Themes of the embittered heart, or so it seems,
That might adorn old songs or courtly shows;
But what cared I that set him on to ride,
I, starved for the bosom of his faery bride?

And then a counter-truth filled out its play,
The Countess Cathleen was the name I gave it;
She, pity-crazed, had given her soul away,
But masterful Heaven had intervened to save it.
I thought my dear must her own soul destroy,
So did fanaticism and hate enslave it,
And this brought forth a dream and soon enough
This dream itself had all my thought and love.

And when the Fool and Blind Man stole the bread
Cuchulain fought the ungovernable sea;
Heart-mysteries there, and yet when all is said
It was the dream itself enchanted me:
Character isolated by a deed
To engross the present and dominate memory.
Players and painted stage took all my love,
And not those things that they were emblems of.

III

Those masterful images because complete
Grew in pure mind, but out of what began?
A mound of refuse or the sweepings of a street,
Old kettles, old bottles, and a broken can,
Old iron, old bones, old rags, that raving slut
Who keeps the till. Now that my ladder's gone,
I must lie down where all the ladders start,
In the foul rag-and-bone shop of the heart.

THE FISHERMAN

Although I can see him still,
The freckled man who goes
To a grey place on a hill
In grey Connemara clothes
At dawn to cast his flies,
It's long since I began
To call up to the eyes
This wise and simple man.
All day I'd looked in the face
What I had hoped 'twould be
To write for my own race
And the reality;
The living men that I hate,
The dead man that I loved,
The craven man in his seat,
The insolent unreproved,
And no knave brought to book
Who has won a drunken cheer,
The witty man and his joke
Aimed at the commonest ear,
The clever man who cries
The catch-cries of the clown,
The beating down of the wise
And great Art beaten down.

Maybe a twelvemonth since
Suddenly I began,
In scorn of this audience,
Imagining a man,
And his sun-freckled face,
And grey Connemara cloth,
Climbing up to a place
Where stone is dark under froth,
And the down-turn of his wrist
When the flies drop in the stream;
A man who does not exist,
A man who is but a dream;
And cried, 'Before I am old
I shall have written him one
Poem maybe as cold
And passionate as the dawn.'

from INCANTATA
In memory of Mary Farl Powers

I thought of you tonight, *a leanbh*, lying there in your long barrow
colder and dumber than a fish by Francisco de Herrera,
as I X-Actoed from a spud the Inca
glyph for a mouth: thought of that first time I saw your pink
spotted torso, distant-near as a nautilus,
when you undid your portfolio, yes indeedy,
and held the print of what looked like a cankered potato
at arm's length – your arms being longer, it seemed, than Lugh's. . . .

I saw you again tonight, in your jump-suit, thin as a rake,
your hand moving in such a deliberate arc
as you ground a lithographic stone
that your hand and the stone blurred to one
and your face blurred into the face of your mother, Betty Wahl,
who took your failing, ink-stained hand
in her failing, ink-stained hand
and together you ground down that stone by sheer force of will. . . .

You must have known already, as we moved from the 'Hurly Burly'
to McDaid's or Riley's,
that something was amiss: I think you even mentioned a
homeopath
as you showed off the great new acid-bath
in the Graphic Studio, and again undid your portfolio
to lay out your latest works; I try to imagine the strain
you must have been under, pretending to be as right as rain
while hearing the bells of a church from some long-flooded valley. . . .

I thought again of how art may be made, as it was by André
Derain,
of nothing more than a turn
in the road where a swallow dips into the mire
or plucks a strand of bloody wool from a strand of barbed wire
in the aftermath of Chickamauga or Culloden
and builds from pain, from misery, from a deep-seated hurt,
a monument to the human heart
that shines like a golden dome among the roofs rain-glazed and
leaden. . . .

Cúl an Tí

Tá Tír na nÓg ar chúl an tí,
Tír álainn trína chéile,
Lucht ceithre chos ag siúl na slí
Gan bróga orthu ná léine,
Gan Béarla acu ná Gaeilge.

Ach fásann clóca ar gach droim
Sa tír seo trína chéile,
Is labhartar teanga ar chúl an tí
Nár thuig aon fhear ach Aesop,
Is tá sé siúd sa chré anois.

Tá cearca ann is sicín,
Is lacha righin mhothaolach,
Is gadhar mór dubh mar namhaid sa tir
Ag drannadh le gach éinne,
Is cat ag crú na gréine.

Sa chúinne thiar tá banc dramhaíl'
Is iontaisí an tsaoil ann,
Coinnleoir, búclaí, seanhata tuí,
Is trúmpa balbh néata,
Is citeal bán mar ghé ann.

Is ann a thagann tincéirí
Go naofa, trína chéile,
Tá gaol acu le cúl an tí,
Is bíd ag iarraidh déirce
Ar chúl gach tí in Éirinn.

Ba mhaith liom bheith ar chúl an tí
Sa doircheacht go déanach
Go bhfeicinn ann ar chuairt gealaí
An t-ollaimhín sin Aesop
Is é ina phúca léannta.

To a Child Dancing in the Wind

Dance there upon the shore;
What need have you to care
For wind or water's roar?
And tumble out your hair
That the salt drops have wet;
Being young you have not known
The fool's triumph, nor yet
Love lost as soon as won,
Nor the best labourer dead
And all the sheaves to bind.
What need have you to dread
The monstrous crying of wind?

from THE TOWER

I pace upon the battlements and stare
On the foundations of a house, or where
Tree, like a sooty finger, starts from the earth;
And send imagination forth
Under the day's declining beam, and call
Images and memories
From ruin or from ancient trees,
For I would ask a question of them all. . . .

It is time that I wrote my will;
I choose upstanding men
That climb the streams until
The fountain leap, and at dawn
Drop their cast at the side
Of dripping stone; I declare
They shall inherit my pride,
The pride of people that were
Bound neither to Cause nor to State,
Neither to slaves that were spat on,
Nor to the tyrants that spat,
The people of Burke and of Grattan
That gave, though free to refuse —
Pride, like that of the morn,
When the headlong light is loose,
Or that of the fabulous horn,
Or that of the sudden shower
When all streams are dry,
Or that of the hour
When the swan must fix his eye
Upon a fading gleam,
Float out upon a long
Last reach of glittering stream
And there sing his last song.
And I declare my faith:
I mock Plotinus' thought
And cry in Plato's teeth,
Death and life were not
Till man made up the whole,

Made lock, stock and barrel
Out of his bitter soul,
Aye, sun and moon and star, all,
And further add to that
That, being dead, we rise,
Dream and so create
Translunar Paradise. . . .

I leave both faith and pride
To young upstanding men
Climbing the mountain-side,
That under bursting dawn
They may drop a fly;
Being of that metal made
Till it was broken by
This sedentary trade.

Now shall I make my soul,
Compelling it to study
In a learned school
Till the wreck of body,
Slow decay of blood,
Testy delirium
Or dull decrepitude,
Or what worse evil come —
The death of friends, or death
Of every brilliant eye
That made a catch in the breath —
Seem but the clouds of the sky
When the horizon fades:
Or a bird's sleepy cry
Among the deepening shades.

1926

Night Feed

This is dawn.
Believe me
This is your season, little daughter:
The moment daisies open,
The hour mercurial rainwater
Makes a mirror for sparrows.
It's time we drowned our sorrows.

I tiptoe in.
I lift you up
Wriggling
In your rosy, zipped sleeper.
Yes this is the hour
For the early bird and me
When finder is keeper.

I crook the bottle.
How you suckle!
This is the best I can be,
Housewife
To this nursery
Where you hold on,
Dear life.

A silt of milk.
The last suck.
And now your eyes are open
Birth-coloured and offended.
Earth wakes.
You go back to sleep.
The feed is ended.

Worms turn.
Stars go in.
Even the moon is losing face.
Poplars stilt for dawn
And we begin
The long fall from grace.
I tuck you in.

She Moved Through the Fair

My young love said to me, "My brothers won't mind,
And my parents won't slight you for your lack of kind."
Then she stepped away from me, and this she did say
"It will not be long, love, till our wedding day."

She stepped away from me and she moved through the fair,
And fondly I watched her go here and go there,
Then she went her way homeward with one star awake,
As the swan in the evening moves over the lake.

The people were saying no two were ere wed
But one had a sorrow that never was said,
And I smiled as she passed with her goods and her gear,
And that was the last that I saw of my dear.

I dreamt it last night that my young love came in,
So softly she entered, her feet made no din;
She came close beside me, and this she did say
"It will not be long, love, till our wedding day."

Death of a Naturalist

All year the flax-dam festered in the heart
Of the townland; green and heavy-headed
Flax had rotted there, weighted down by huge sods.
Daily it sweltered in the punishing sun.
Bubbles gargled delicately, bluebottles
Wove a strong gauze of sound around the smell.
There were dragonflies, spotted butterflies,
But best of all was the warm thick slobber
Of frogspawn that grew like clotted water
In the shade of the banks. Here, every spring
I would fill jampotfuls of the jellied
Specks to range on window-sills at home,
On shelves at school, and wait and watch until
The fattening dots burst into nimble —
Swimming tadpoles. Miss Walls would tell us how
The daddy frog was called a bullfrog
And how he croaked and how the mammy frog
Laid hundreds of little eggs and this was
Frogspawn. You could tell the weather by frogs too
For they were yellow in the sun and brown
In rain.

Then one hot day when fields were rank
With cowdung in the grass the angry frogs
Invaded the flax-dam; I ducked through hedges
To a coarse croaking that I had not heard
Before. The air was thick with a bass chorus.
Right down the dam gross-bellied frogs were cocked
On sods; their loose necks pulsed like sails. Some hopped:
The slap and plop were obscene threats. Some sat
Poised like mud grenades, their blunt heads farting.
I sickened, turned, and ran. The great slime kings
Were gathered there for vengeance and I knew
That if I dipped my hand the spawn would clutch it.

Requiem for the Croppies

The pockets of our greatcoats full of barley —
No kitchens on the run, no striking camp —
We moved quick and sudden in our own country.
The priest lay behind ditches with the tramp.
A people, hardly marching — on the hike —
We found new tactics happening each day:
We'd cut through reins and rider with the pike
And stampede cattle into infantry,
Then retreat through hedges where cavalry must be thrown.
Until, on Vinegar Hill, the fatal conclave.
Terraced thousands died, shaking scythes at cannon.
The hillside blushed, soaked in our broken wave.
They buried us without shroud or coffin
And in August the barley grew up out of the grave.

AUTUMN JOURNAL

Close and slow, summer is ending in Hampshire,
Ebbing away down ramps of shaven lawn where close-clipped yew
Insulates the lives of retired generals and admirals
And the spyglasses hung in the hall and the prayer-books ready in
the pew
And August going out to the tin trumpets of nasturtiums
And the sunflowers' Salvation Army blare of brass
And the spinster sitting in a deck-chair picking up stitches
Not raising her eyes to the noise of the 'planes that pass
Northward from Lee-on-Solent. Macrocarpa and cypress
And roses on a rustic trellis and mulberry trees
And bacon and eggs in a silver dish for breakfast
And all the inherited assets of bodily ease
And all the inherited worries, rheumatism and taxes,
And whether Stella will marry and what to do with Dick
And the branch of the family that lost their money in Hatry
And the passing of the *Morning Post* and of life's climacteric
And the growth of vulgarity, cars that pass the gate-lodge
And crowds undressing on the beach
And the hiking cockney lovers with thoughts directed
Neither to God nor Nation but each to each.
But the home is still a sanctum under the pelmets,
All quiet on the Family Front,
Farmyard noises across the fields at evening
While the trucks of the Southern Railway dawdle . . . shunt
Into poppy sidings for the night - night which knows no passion
No assault of hands or tongue
For all is old as flint or chalk or pine-needles
And the rebels and the young
Have taken the train to town or the two-seater
Unravelling rails or road,
Losing the thread deliberately behind them—
Autumnal palinode.
And I am in the train too now and summer is going
South as I go north
Bound for the dead leaves falling, the burning bonfire,
The dying that brings forth
The harder life, revealing the trees' girders,
The frost that kills the germs of *laissez-faire*;

West Meon, Tisted, Farnham, Woking, Weybridge,
Then London's packed and stale and pregnant air
My dog, a symbol of the abandoned order,
Lies on the carriage floor,
Her eyes inept and glamorous as a film star's,
Who wants to live, i.e. wants more
Presents, jewellery, furs, gadgets, solicitations
As if to live were not
Following the curve of a planet or controlled water
But a leap in the dark, a tangent, a stray shot.
It is this we learn after so many failures,
The building of castles in sand, of queens in snow,
That we cannot make any corner in life or in life's beauty,
That no river is a river which does not flow.
Surbiton, and a woman gets in, painted
With dyed hair but a ladder in her stocking and eyes
Patient beneath the calculated lashes,
Inured for ever to surprise;
And the train's rhythm becomes the *ad nauseam* repetition
Of every tired aubade and maudlin madrigal,
The faded airs of sexual attraction
Wandering like dead leaves along a warehouse wall:
'I loved my love with a platform ticket,
A jazz song,
A handbag, a pair of stockings of Paris Sand —
I loved her long.
I loved her between the lines and against the clock,
Not until death
But till life did us part I loved her with paper money
And with whisky on the breath.
I loved her with peacock's eyes and the wares of Carthage,
With glass and gloves and gold and a powder puff
With blasphemy, camaraderie, and bravado
And lots of other stuff.
I loved my love with the wings of angels
Dipped in henna, unearthly red,
With my office hours, with flowers and sirens,
With my budget, my latchkey, and my daily bread.'
And so to London and down the ever-moving Stairs
Where a warm wind blows the bodies of men together
And blows apart their complexes and cares.

DUBLIN

Grey brick upon brick,
Declamatory bronze
On sombre pedestals —
O'Connell, Grattan, Moore —
And the brewery tugs and the swans
On the balustraded stream
And the bare bones of a fanlight
Over a hungry door
And the air soft on the cheek
And porter running from the taps
With a head of yellow cream
And Nelson on his pillar
Watching his world collapse.

This was never my town,
I was not born nor bred
Nor schooled here and she will not
Have me alive or dead
But yet she holds my mind
With her seedy elegance,
With her gentle veils of rain
And all her ghosts that walk
And all that hide behind
Her Georgian façades —
The catcalls and the pain,
The glamour of her squalor,
The bravado of her talk.

The lights jig in the river
With a concertina movement
And the sun comes up in the morning
Like barley-sugar on the water
And the mist on the Wicklow hills
Is close, as close
As the peasantry were to the landlord,
As the Irish to the Anglo-Irish,
As the killer is close one moment
To the man he kills,
Or as the moment itself
Is close to the next moment.

She is not an Irish town
And she is not English,
Historic with guns and vermin
And the cold renown
Of a fragment of Church latin,
Of an oratorical phrase.
But O the days are soft,
Soft enough to forget
The lesson better learnt,
The bullet on the wet
Streets, the crooked deal,
The steel behind the laugh,
The Four Courts, burnt.

Fort of the Dane,
Garrison of the Saxon,
Augustan capital
Of a Gaelic nation,
Appropriating all
The alien brought,
You give me time for thought
And by a juggler's trick
You poise the toppling hour —
O greyness run to flower,
Grey stone, grey water
And brick upon grey brick.

DARK ROSALEEN

O, my Dark Rosaleen,
Do not sigh, do not weep!
The priests are on the ocean green,
They march along the Deep.
There's wine from the royal Pope,
Upon the ocean green;
And Spanish ale shall give you hope,
My Dark Rosaleen!
My own Rosaleen!
Shall glad your heart, shall give you hope,
Shall give you health, and help, and hope,
My Dark Rosaleen!

Over hills, and through dales,
Have I roamed for your sake;
All yesterday I sailed with sails
On river and on lake.
The Erne, at its highest flood,
I dashed across unseen,
For there was lightning in my blood,
My Dark Rosaleen!
My own Rosaleen!
Oh! there was lightning in my blood,
Red lightning lightened through my blood,
My Dark Rosaleen!

All day long, in unrest,
To and fro, do I move.
The very soul within my breast
Is wasted for you, love!
The heart in my bosom faints
To think of you, my Queen,
My life of life, my saint of saints,
My Dark Rosaleen!
My own Rosaleen!
To hear your sweet and sad complaints,
My life, my love, my saint of saints,
My Dark Rosaleen!

Woe and pain, pain and woe,
Are my lot, night and noon,
To see your bright face clouded so,
Like to the mournful moon.
But yet will I rear your throne
Again in golden sheen;
'Tis you shall reign, shall reign alone,
My Dark Rosaleen!
My own Rosaleen!
'Tis you shall have the golden throne,
'Tis you shall reign, and reign alone,
My Dark Rosaleen!

Over dews, over sands,
Will I fly, for your weal:
Your holy, delicate white hands
Shall girdle me with steel.
At home in your emerald bowers,
From morning's dawn till e'en,
You'll pray for me, my flower of flowers,
My Dark Rosaleen!
My fond Rosaleen!
You'll think of me through daylight's hours,
My virgin flower, my flower of flowers,
My Dark Rosaleen!

I could scale the blue air,
I could plough the high hills,
Oh, I could kneel all night in prayer,
To heal your many ills!
And one beamy smile from you
Would float like light between
My toils and me, my own, my true,
My Dark Rosaleen!
My fond Rosaleen!
Would give me life and soul anew,
A second life, a soul anew,
My dark Rosaleen!

O! the Erne shall run red
With redundance of blood,
The earth shall rock beneath our tread,
And flames wrap hill and wood,
And gun-peal, and slogan cry
Wake many a glen serene,
Ere you shall fade, ere you shall die,
My Dark Rosaleen!
My own Rosaleen!
The Judgement Hour must first be nigh,
Ere you can fade, ere you can die,
My Dark Rosaleen!

THE MEETING OF THE WATERS

There is not in the wide world a valley so sweet
As that vale in whose bosom the bright waters meet;
Oh! the last rays of feeling and life must depart,
Ere the bloom of that valley shall fade from my heart.

Yet it *was* not that Nature had shed o'er the scene
Her purest of crystal and brightest of green;
'Twas *not* her soft magic of streamlet or hill,
Oh! no, — it was something more exquisite still.

'Twas that friends, the belov'd of my bosom, were near,
Who made every dear scene of enchantment more dear,
And who felt how the best charms of nature improve,
When we see them reflected from looks that we love.

Sweet vale of Avoca! how calm could I rest
In thy bosom of shade, with the friends I love best,
Where the storms that we feel in this cold world should cease,
And our hearts, like thy waters, be mingled in peace.

BEAN TSLÉIBHE AG CAOINEADH A MIC

Brón ar an mbás, is é dhubh mo chroí-se,
D'fhuadaigh mo ghrá is d'fhág mé cloíte,
Gan charaid gan chompánach faoi dhíon mo thí-se
Ach an léan so im' lár, is mé ag caoineadh.

Ag gabháil an tsléibhe dhom tráthnóna
Do labhair an éanlaith lion go brónach,
Do labhair an naosc binn 's an crotach glórach
Ag faisnéis domgur éag mo stórach.

Do ghlaoigh mé ort is do ghlór níor chualas,
Do ghlaoigh mé arís is freagra ní bhfuaireas,
Do phóg mé do bhéal, is a Dhia, nárbh fhuar é!
Och, is fuar í do leaba sla chillín uaigneach.

'S a uaigh fhód-ghlas ina bhfuil mo leanbh,
A uaigh chaol bheag, ós tú a leaba,
Mo bheannacht ort, 's na mílte beannacht
Ar na fódaibh glasa atá os cionn mo pheata.

Brón ar an mbás, ní féidir a shéanadh,
Leagann sé úr is críon le chéile, —
'S a mhaicín mhánla, is é mo chéasadh
Do cholainn chaomh bheith ag déanamh créafóig.

Poet's own translation page 145.

The Ballad of Father Gilligan

The old priest Peter Gilligan
Was weary night and day;
For half his flock were in their beds,
Or under green sods lay.

Once, while he nodded on a chair,
At the moth-hour of eve,
Another poor man sent for him,
And he began to grieve.

'I have no rest, nor joy, nor peace,
For people die and die';
And after cried he, 'God forgive!
My body spake, not I!'

He knelt, and leaning on the chair
He prayed and fell asleep;
And the moth-hour went from the fields,
And stars began to peep.

They slowly into millions grew,
And leaves shook in the wind;
And God covered the world with shade,
And whispered to mankind.

Upon the time of sparrow-chirp
When the moths came once more,
The old priest Peter Gilligan
Stood upright on the floor.

'Mavrone, mavrone! the man has died
While I slept on the chair';
He roused his horse out of its sleep,
And rode with little care.

He rode now as he never rode,
By rocky lane and fen;
The sick man's wife opened the door:
'Father! you come again!'

'And is the poor man dead?' he cried.
'He died an hour ago.'
The old priest Peter Gilligan
In grief swayed to and fro.

'When you were gone, he turned and died
As merry as a bird.'
The old priest Peter Gilligan
He knelt him at that word.

'He Who hath made the night of stars
For souls who tire and bleed,
Sent one of His great angels down
To help me in my need.

'He Who is wrapped in purple robes,
With planets in His care,
Had pity on the least of things
Asleep upon a chair.'

Red Hanrahan's Song about Ireland

The old brown thorn-trees break in two high over Cummen
      Strand,
Under a bitter black wind that blows from the left hand;
Our courage breaks like an old tree in a black wind and dies,
But we have hidden in our hearts the flame out of the eyes
Of Cathleen, the daughter of Houlihan.

The wind has bundled up the clouds high over Knocknarea,
And thrown the thunder on the stones for all that Maeve can say.
Angers that are like noisy clouds have set our hearts abeat;
But we have all bent low and low and kissed the quiet feet
Of Cathleen, the daughter of Houlihan.

The yellow pool has overflowed high up on Clooth-na-Bare,
For the wet winds are blowing out of the clinging air;
Like heavy flooded waters out bodies and our blood;
But purer than a tall candle before the Holy Rood
Is Cathleen, the daughter of Houlihan.

The Fairies

Up the airy mountain,
Down the rushy glen,
We daren't go a-hunting
For fear of little men;
Wee folk, good folk,
Trooping all together;
Green jacket, red cap,
And white owl's feather!

Down along the rocky shore
Some make their home—
They live on crispy pancakes
Of yellow tide-foam;
Some in the reeds
Of the black mountain lake,
With frogs for their watch-dogs,
All night awake.

High on the hill-top
The old King sits;
He is now so old and grey
He's nigh lost his wits.
With a bridge of white mist
Columbkill he crosses,
On his stately journeys
From Slieveleague to Rosses;
Or going up with music
On cold starry nights,
To sup with the Queen
Of the gay Northern Lights.

They stole little Bridget
For seven years long;
When she came down again
Her friends were all gone.
They took her lightly back,
Between the night and morrow;
They thought that she was fast asleep,

But she was dead with sorrow.
They have kept her ever since
Deep within the lake,
On a bed of flag-leaves,
Watching till she wake.

By the craggy hill-side,
Through the mosses bare,
They have planted thorn-trees
For pleasure here and there.
Is any man so daring
As dig one up in spite,
He shall find their sharpest thorns
In his bed at night.

Up the airy mountain,
Down the rushy glen,
We daren't go a-hunting
For fear of little men;
Wee folk, good folk,
Trooping all together;
Green jacket, red cap,
And white owl's feather!

Pangur Bán

I and Pangur Bán, my cat,
'Tis a like task we are at;
Hunting mice is his delight,
Hunting words I sit all night.

Better far than praise of men
'Tis to sit with book and pen;
Pangur bears me no ill will,
He too plies his simple skill.

'Tis a merry thing to see
At our tasks how glad are we,
When at home we sit and find
Entertainment to our mind.

Oftentimes a mouse will stray
In the hero Pangur's way;
Oftentimes my keen thought set
Takes a meaning in its net.

'Gainst the wall he sets his eye
Full and fierce and sharp and sly;
'Gainst the wall of knowledge I
All my little wisdom try.

When a mouse darts from its den,
O how glad is Pangur then!
O what gladness do I prove
When I solve the doubts I love!

So in peace our tasks we ply,
Pangur Bán, my cat and I;
In our hearts we find our bliss,
I have mine and he has his.

Practice every day has made
Pangur perfect in his trade;
I get wisdom day and night
Turning darkness into light.

FOLLOWER

My father worked with a horse-plough,
His shoulders globed like a full sail strung
Between the shafts and the furrow.
The horses strained at his clicking tongue.

An expert. He would set the wing
And fit the bright steel-pointed sock.
The sod rolled over without breaking.
At the headrig, with a single pluck

Of reins, the sweating team turned round
And back into the land. His eye
Narrowed and angled at the ground,
Mapping the furrow exactly.

I stumbled in his hobnailed wake,
Fell sometimes on the polished sod;
Sometimes he rode me on his back
Dipping and rising to his plod.

I wanted to grow up and plough,
To close one eye, stiffen my arm.
All I ever did was follow
In his broad shadow round the farm.

I was a nuisance, tripping, falling,
Yapping always. But today
It is my father who keeps stumbling
Behind me, and will not go away.

PADRAIC O'CONAIRE, GAELIC STORYTELLER

They've paid the last respects in sad tobacco
And silent is this wakehouse in its haze;
They've paid the last respects; and now their whiskey
Flings laughing words on mouths of prayer and praise;
And so young couples huddle by the gables,
O let them grope home through the hedgy night —
Alone I'll mourn my old friend, while the cold dawn
Thins out the holy candlelight.

Respects are paid to one loved by the people;
Ah, was he not — among our mighty poor —
The sudden wealth cast on those pools of darkness,
Those bearing, just, a star's faint signature;
And so he was to me, close friend, near brother,
Dear Padraic of the wide and sea-cold eyes—
So lovable, so courteous and noble,
The very West was in his soft replies.

They'll miss his heavy stick and stride in Wicklow —
His story-talking down Winetavern Street
Where old men sitting in the wizen daylight
Have kept an edge upon his gentle wit;
While women on the grassy streets of Galway,
Who hearken for his passing — but in vain,
Shall hardly tell his step as shadows vanish
Through archways of forgotten Spain.

Ah, they'll say: Padraic's gone again exploring;
But now down glens of brightness, O he'll find
An alehouse overflowing with wise Gaelic
That's braced in vigour by the bardic mind,
And there his thoughts shall find their own forefathers —
In minds to whom our heights of race belong,
In crafty men, who ribbed a ship or turned
The secret joinery of song.

Alas, death mars the parchment of his forehead;
And yet for him, I know, the earth is mild —
The windy fidgets of September grasses
Can never tease a mind that loved the wild;
So drink his peace — this grey juice of the barley
Runs with a light that ever pleased his eye —
While old flames nod and gossip on the hearthstone
And only the young winds cry.

To my Daughter Betty, the Gift of God.

In wiser days, my darling rosebud, blown
To beauty proud as was your mother's prime,
In that desired, delayed, incredible time,
You'll ask why I abandoned you, my own,
And the dear heart that was your baby throne,
To dice with death. And oh! They'll give you rhyme
And reason: some will call the thing sublime,
And some decry it in a knowing tone.
So here, while the mad guns curse overhead,
And tired men sigh with mud for couch and floor,
Know that we fools, now with the foolish dead,
Died not for flag, nor King, nor Emperor,
But for a dream, born in a herdsman's shed,
And for the secret Scripture of the poor.

In the field, before Guillemont, Somme, September 4, 1916.

The Fool

Since the wise men have not spoken, I speak that am only a fool;
A fool that hath loved his folly,
Yea, more than the wise men their books or their counting houses
or their quiet homes
Or their fame in men's mouths;
A fool that in all his days hath done never a prudent thing,
Never hath counted the cost, nor recked if another reaped
The fruit of his mighty sowing, content scatter the seed;

A fool that is unrepentant, and that soon at the end of all
Shall laugh in his lonely heart as the ripe ears fall to the reaping-
hooks
And the poor are filled that were empty,
Tho' he go hungry.

I have squandered the splendid years that the Lord God gave to
my youth
In attempting impossible things, deeming them alone worth the
toil.
Was it folly or grace? Not men shall judge me, but God.

I have squandered the splendid years:
Lord, if I had the years I would squander them over again,
Aye, fling them from me!
For this I have heard in my heart, that a man shall scatter not
hoard,
Shall do the deed of to-day, nor take thought of to-morrow's teen,
Shall not bargain or huxter with God; or was it a jest of Christ's
And is this my sin before men; to have taken Him at His word?

The lawyers have sat in council, the men with the keen, long faces,
And said, 'This man is a fool,' and others have said, 'He
blasphemeth';
And the wise have pitied the fool that hath striven to give a life
In the world of time and space among the bulks of actual things,
To a dream that was dreamed in the heart, and that only the heart
could hold.

O wise men, riddle me this: what if the dream come true?
What if the dream come true? and if millions unborn shall dwell
In the house that I shaped in my heart, the noble house of my
thought?
Lord, I have staked my soul, I have staked the lives of my kin
On the truth of Thy dreadful word. Do not remember my failures,
But remember this my faith.

And so I speak.
Yea, ere my hot youth pass, I speak to my people and say:
Ye shall be foolish as I; ye shall scatter, not save;
Ye shall venture your all, lest ye lose what is more than all;
Ye shall call for a miracle, taking Christ at His word.
And for this I will answer, O people, answer here and hereafter,
O people that I have loved shall we not answer together?

The Splendour of God

The drunken stars stagger across the sky,
The moon wavers and sways like a windblown bud,
Beneath my feet the earth like drifting scud
Lapses and slides, wallows and shoots on high;
Immovable things start suddenly flying by,
The city shakes and quavers, a city of mud
And ooze — a brawling cataract is my blood
Of molten metal and fire — like God am I.

When God crushes his passion-fruit for our thirst
And the universe totters — I have burst the grape
Of the world, and let its powerful blood escape
Untasted — crying whether my vision durst
See God's high glory in a girl's soft shape —
God! Is my worship blesséd or accurst?

Sheep and Lambs

All in the April evening,
April airs were abroad,
The sheep with their little lambs
Passed me by on the road.

The sheep with their little lambs
Passed me by on the road;
All in the April evening
I thought on the Lamb of God.

The lambs were weary, and crying
With a weak, human cry.
I thought on the Lamb of God
Going meekly to die.

Up in the blue, blue mountains
Dewy pastures are sweet;
Rest for the little bodies,
Rest for the little feet,

But for the Lamb of God,
Up on the hilltop green,
Only a cross of shame
Two stark crosses between.

All in the April evening,
April airs were abroad;
I saw the sheep with their lambs,
And thought on the Lamb of God.

Broken Dreams

There is grey in your hair.
Young men no longer suddenly catch their breath
When you are passing;
But maybe some old gaffer mutters a blessing
Because it was your prayer
Recovered him upon the bed of death.
For your sole sake - that all heart's ache have known,
And given to others all heart's ache,
From meagre girlhood's putting on
Burdensome beauty - for your sole sake
Heaven has put away the stroke of her doom,
So great her portion in that peace you make
By merely walking in a room.

Your beauty can but leave among us
Vague memories, nothing but memories.
A young man when the old men are done talking
Will say to an old man, 'Tell me of that lady
The poet stubborn with his passion sang us
When age might well have chilled his blood.'

Vague memories, nothing but memories,
But in the grave all, all, shall be renewed.
The certainty that I shall see that lady
Leaning or standing or walking
In the first loveliness of womanhood,
And with the fervour of my youthful eyes,
Has set me muttering like a fool.

You are more beautiful than any one,
And yet your body had a flaw:
Your small hands were not beautiful,
And I am afraid that you will run
And paddle to the wrist
In that mysterious, always brimming lake
Where those that have obeyed the holy law
Paddle and are perfect. Leave unchanged
The hands that I have kissed,
For old sake's sake.

The last stroke of midnight dies.
All day in the one chair
From dream to dream and rhyme to rhyme I have ranged
In rambling talk with an image of air:
Vague memories, nothing but memories.

DOWN BY THE SALLEY GARDENS

Down by the salley gardens my love and I did meet;
She passed the salley gardens with little snow-white feet.
She bid me take love easy, as the leaves grow on the tree;
But I, being young and foolish, with her would not agree.

In a field by the river my love and I did stand,
And on my leaning shoulder she laid her snow-white hand.
She bid me take life easy, as the grass grows on the weirs;
But I was young and foolish, and now am full of tears.

You waves, though you dance by my feet like children at play,
Though you glow and you glance, though you purr and you dart;
In the Junes that were warmer than these are, the waves were more
gay,
When I was a boy with never a crack in my heart.

The herring are not in the tides as they were of old
My sorrow! for many a creak gave the creel in the cart
That carried the take to Sligo town to be sold,
When I was a boy with never a crack in my heart.

And ah, you proud maiden, you are not so fair when his oar
Is heard on the water, as they were, the proud and apart,
Who paced in the eve by the nets on the pebbly shore,
When I was a boy with never a crack in my heart.

UNDER BEN BULBEN

I

Swear by what the sages spoke
Round the Mareotic Lake
That the Witch of Atlas knew,
Spoke and set the cocks a-crow.

Swear by those horsemen, by those women
Complexion and form prove superhuman,
That pale, long-visaged company
That air in immortality
Completeness of their passions won;
Now they ride the wintry dawn
Where Ben Bulben sets the scene.

Here's the gist of what they mean.

II

Many times man lives and dies
Between his two eternities,
That of race and that of soul,
And ancient Ireland knew it all.
Whether man die in his bed
Or the rifle knock him dead,
A brief parting from those dear
Is the worst man has to fear,
Though grave-diggers' toil is long,
Sharp their spades, their muscles strong,
They but thrust their buried men
Back in the human mind again.

III

You that Mitchel's prayer have heard.
'Send war in our time, O Lord!'
Know that when all words are said
And a man is fighting mad,
Something drops from eyes long blind,
He completes his partial mind,
For an instant stands at ease,

Laughs aloud, his heart at peace.
Even the wisest man grows tense
With some sort of violence
Before he can accomplish fate,
Know his work or choose his mate.

IV

Poet and sculptor, do the work,
Nor let the modish painter shirk
What his great forefathers did,
Bring the soul of man to God,
Make him fill the cradles right.

Measurement began our might:
Forms a stark Egyptian thought,
Forms that gentler Phidias wrought.
Michael Angelo left a proof
On the Sistine Chapel roof,
Where but half-awakened Adam
Can disturb globe-trotting Madam
Till her bowels are in heat,
Proof that there's a purpose set
Before the secret working mind:
Profane perfection of mankind.

Quattrocento put in paint
On backgrounds for a God or Saint
Gardens where a soul's at ease;
Where everything that meets the eye,
Flowers and grass and cloudless sky,
Resemble forms that are or seem
When sleepers wake and yet still dream,
And when it's vanished still declare,
With only bed and bedstead there,
That heavens have opened.
Gyres run on;
When that greater dream had gone
Calvert and Wilson, Blake and Claude,
Prepared a rest for the people of God,
Palmer's phrase, but after that
Confusion fell upon our thought.

V

Irish poets, learn your trade,
Sing whatever is well made,
Scorn the sort now growing up
All out of shape from toe to top,
Their unremembering hearts and heads
Base-born products of base beds.
Sing the peasantry, and then
Hard-riding country gentlemen,
The holiness of monks, and after
Porter-drinkers' randy laughter;
Sing the lords and ladies gay
That were beaten into the clay
Through seven heroic centuries;
Cast your mind on other days
That we in coming days may be
Still the indomitable Irishry.

VI

Under bare Ben Bulben's head
In Drumcliff churchyard Yeats is laid.
An ancestor was rector there
Long years ago, a church stands near,
By the road an ancient cross.
No marble, no conventional phrase;
On limestone quarried near the spot
By his command these words are cut:

Cast a cold eye
On life, on death.
Horseman, pass by!

September 4, 1938.

An Long

Tháinig long ó Valparaiso,
Scaoileadh téad a seol sa chuan;
Chuir a hainm dom i gcuimhne
Ríocht na gréine, tír na mbua.

"Gluais," ar sí, "ar thuras fada
Liom ó scamall is ó cheo;
Tá fé shleasaibh gorm-Andes
Cathair scáfar, glé mar sheod."

Ach bhíos óg is ní imeoinnse,
Am an dóchais, tús mo shaoil;
Chreideas fós go raibh i ndán dom
Iontaisí na ndán 's na scéal.

Ghluais an long thar linntibh mara
Fad' ó shin 's a crann mar ór,
Scríobh a scéal ar phár na hoíche,
Ard i rian na réiltean mór.

Fillfidh sí arís chugam, áfach;
Chífead cathair bhán fén sléibh
Le hais Mara na Síochána —
Creidim fós beagnach, a Dhé.

Translation Theo Dorgan page 146.

A Cradle Song

O, men from the fields!
Come gently within.
Tread softly, softly,
O! men coming in.

Mavourneen is going
From me and from you,
Where Mary will fold him
With mantle of blue!

From reek of the smoke
And cold of the floor,
And the peering of things
Across the half-door.

O, men from the fields!
Soft, softly come through —
Mary puts round him
Her mantle of blue.

A Drover

To Meath of the pastures,
From wet hills by the sea,
Through Leitrim and Longford,
Go my cattle and me.

I hear in the darkness
Their slipping and breathing—
I name them the by-ways
They're to pass without heeding;

Then the wet, winding roads,
Brown bogs with black water,
And my thoughts on white ships
And the King o' Spain's daughter.

O farmer, strong farmer!
You can spend at the fair,
But your face you must turn
To your crops and your care;

And soldiers, red soldiers!
You've seen many lands,
But you walk two by two,
And by captain's commands!

O the smell of the beasts,
The wet wind in the morn,
And the proud and hard earth
Never broken for corn!

And the crowds at the fair,
The herds loosened and blind,
Loud woods and dark faces,
And the wild blood behind!

(O strong men with your best
I would strive breast to breast,
I could quiet your herds
With my words, with my words!)

I will bring you, my kine,
Where there's grass to the knee,
But you'll think of scant croppings
Harsh with salt of the sea.

from WOODMAN

Not second sight so much
as the eyes of deep experience
enabled my father to see
through to the heart of trees.

He discerned the ringed
grain, coopage of winters,
summers contained, and understood
how it would run in terms

of the flat plank, the curved
contours of the hurley stick.
He could tell how many hurleys
per tree, and was alert

to the knot's mischief, the bind
of broken growth. Tree-sap
would come into his eyes,
he'd see a way to seasoning. . . .

Was it the shaping, his arms
framing a diamond space,
shortening and elongating
in their to-fro concurrence

with the plane, brought patience
as he leaned in at the bench
salted with his sweat?
Or was it the way ends met?

The pencilled delineation
of a pattern along a plank —
his solitary superimposition.
He'd proceed from its guideline

to carve out a freedom
for the hurley asleep in ash,
with such clarity of vision
that, textured and unique

as any hand-wrought thing,
it would sing its praise
and, as a consequence, his own,
on fields of furthest Sunday.

At night, hunched till late,
wedging myself into the white
spaces between the lines,
I'd hear him pronounce my fate.

And maybe words *will* be the end
of me yet, nothing transmuted,
the page still as it was,
pulped straw, rags and wood,

the man still uncelebrated.
Dublin offered a roomier space,
heyday and high noon,
my own mode of expression.

The woods were mentioned
by letter now, casual remarks
about *lots* and *stands*
and *cubic feet, foresters*

and *fellings* and *old estates,*
dropped to my new address,
the wistful light of boyhood
leaf-filtered, ever at a slant.

Stay at this job long enough
And it'll kill you, father said.
He decided to follow
his body's advice and retire,

allowing for one last wood.
Careful cuttings, sizings-up.
His final tree fell
in need of a high, angled lop.

The prophecy he had made
came bitterly true as he took
one small step back, yet far
from here, and forever.

from CHRISTMAS DAY

. . . 'Tea or coffee, Mr D?'
'I'm all right, Frank.'
'For the love of Scobie, Paul,
Will you stop being so polite -
It does not become you.
The horriblest git in Ireland
Is that murderous little archimatect,
Carleton O'Flaherty.
We are agreed on that.
That baldy little satyr
From Mulhuddart, ensconced
In his solar pad in Shrewsbury Road
With his two Doberman Pinschers
And his five wives
Who all went to Mount Anville.
We all went to Mount Anville
You can hear them screeching
From the rooftops of Shrewsbury Road
We all went to Mount Anville
And took a degree in sociology
In UCD.
You could do with a little
Murder in your soul, Paul.
Now, you can have any kind
Of coffee your intestines crave:
Maxwell House Instantaneous
Or Bewley's Groundswoman —
I do a mischievous
Blend of slinky Costa Rica
And husky French Roast —
Or you can have chaste Barry's Tea
Or Early Grey
Or Tardy Breakfast
Or even Breaking Orange Pekoe
Or Twig Smithereens.'
'I'll have a cup of hot water.'
'By the hokey, Mr D,
You are an exotic creature.'

When I fish out from my breast pocket
A teabag of herbal —
Rose Hip —
And slip it
Into the cup of hot water
Frank raises his eyebrows
Higher than I have seen
Anyone's eyebrows ever go —
So high I begin to see
His eyebrows scuttling about
The wainscotting of his scalp
Between his forehead and hairline.
When I scoop out the teabag
And drop it in the ashtray —
An Eiffel Tower ashtray from Paris —
He snatches it and holds it up
To the light like a mad cat
With a mouse by the tail,
His eyes all teeth a-glittery;
Swinging my teabag
By its limp G-string;
'What have we got here?'
After a brief, hot struggle
With my anger and shame,
My whining *amour propre*,
I see that he is not a catatonic cat
But a fifty-year-old child
Luxuriating in astoundment —
He has never before in his life seen
A herbal tea-drinking male of the species.
'Rose Hip – you don't tell me!'
He murmurs over and over
Like Lord Tennyson making love
To his chambermaid – 'Rose Hip!' . . .

Going Home to Mayo,
Winter, 1949

Leaving behind us the alien, foreign city of Dublin
My father drove through the night in an old Ford Anglia,
His five-year-old son in the seat beside him,
The rexine seat of red leatherette,
And a yellow moon peered in through the windscreen.
'Daddy, Daddy,' I cried, 'Pass out the moon,'
But no matter how hard he drove he could not pass out the moon.
Each town we passed through was another milestone
And their names were magic passwords into eternity:
Kilcock, Kinnegad, Strokestown, Elphin,
Tarmonbarry, Tulsk, Ballaghaderreen, Ballavarry;
Now we were in Mayo and the next stop was Turlough,
The village of Turlough in the heartland of Mayo,
And my father's mother's house, all oil-lamps and women,
And my bedroom over the public bar below,
And in the morning cattle-cries and cock-crows:
Life's seemingly seamless garment gorgeously rent
By their screeches and bellowings. And in the evenings
I walked with my father in the high grass down by the river
Talking with him - an unheard-of thing in the city.

But home was not home and the moon could be no more
outflanked
Than the daylight nightmare of Dublin city:
Back down along the canal we chugged into the city
And each lock-gate tolled our mutual doom;
And railings and palings and asphalt and traffic-lights,
And blocks after blocks of so-called 'new' tenements
Thousands of crosses of loneliness planted
In the narrowing grave of the life of the father;
In the wide, wide cemetery of the boy's childhood.

Death of an Irishwoman

Ignorant, in the sense
she ate monotonous food
and thought the world was flat,
and pagan, in the sense
she knew the things that moved
at night were neither dogs nor cats
but *púcas* and darkfaced men,
she nevertheless had fierce pride.
But sentenced in the end
to eat thin diminishing porridge
in a stone-cold kitchen
she clenched her brittle hands
around a world
she could not understand.
I loved her from the day she died.

She was a summer dance at the crossroads.
She was a cardgame where a nose was broken.
She was a song that nobody sings.
She was a house ransacked by soldiers.
She was a language seldom spoken.
She was a child's purse, full of useless things.

Postscript

And some time make the time to drive out west
Into County Clare, along the Flaggy Shore,
In September or October, when the wind
And the light are working off each other
So that the ocean on one side is wild
With foam and glitter, and inland among stones
The surface of a slate-grey lake is lit
By the earthed lightning of a flock of swans,
Their feathers roughed and ruffling, white on white,
Their fully grown headstrong-looking heads
Tucked or cresting or busy underwater.
Useless to think you'll park and capture it
More thoroughly. You are neither here nor there,
A hurry through which known and strange things pass
As big soft buffetings come at the car sideways
And catch the heart off guard and blow it open.

from STATION ISLAND

A hurry of bell-notes
flew over morning hush
and water-blistered cornfields,
an escaped ringing
that stopped as quickly

as it started. *Sunday*,
the silence breathed
and could not settle back
for a man had appeared
at the side of the field

with a bow-saw, held
stiffly up like a lyre.
He moved and stopped to gaze
up into hazel bushes,
angled his saw in,

pulled back to gaze again
and move on to the next.
'I know you, Simon Sweeney,
for an old Sabbath-breaker
who has been dead for years.'

'Damn all you know,' he said,
his eye still on the hedge
and not turning his head.
'I was your mystery man
and am again this morning.

Through gaps in the bushes,
your First Communion face
would watch me cutting timber.
When cut or broken limbs
of trees went yellow, when

woodsmoke sharpened air
or ditches rustled

you sensed my trail there
as if it had been sprayed.
It left you half afraid.

When they bade you listen
in the bedroom dark
to wind and rain in the trees
and think of tinkers camped
under a heeled-up cart

you shut your eyes and saw
a wet axle and spokes
in moonlight, and me
streaming from the shower,
headed for your door.'

Sunlight broke in the hazels,
the quick bell-notes began
a second time. I turned
at another sound:
a crowd of shawled women

were wading the young corn,
their skirts brushing softly.
Their motion saddened morning.
It whispered to the silence,
'Pray for us, pray for us,'

it conjured through the air
until the field was full
of half-remembered faces,
a loosed congregation
that straggled past and on.

As I drew behind them
I was a fasted pilgrim,
light-headed, leaving home
to face into my station.
'Stay clear of all processions!'

Sweeney shouted at me,
but the murmur of the crowd
and their feet slushing through
the tender, bladed growth
had opened a drugged path

I was set upon.
I trailed those early-risers
fallen into step
before the smokes were up.
The quick bell rang again. . . .

Father and Son

Only last week, walking the hushed fields
Of our most lovely Meath, now thinned by November,
I came to where the road from Laracor leads
To the Boyne river — that seemed more lake than river,
Stretched in uneasy light and stript of reeds.

And walking longside an old weir
Of my people's, where nothing stirs — only the shadowed
Leaden flight of a heron up the lean air —
I went unmanly with grief, knowing how my father,
Happy though captive in years, walked last with me there.

Yes, happy in Meath with me for a day
He walked, taking stock of herds hid in their own breathing;
And naming colts, gusty as wind, once steered by his hand,
Lightnings winked in the eyes that were half shy in greeting
Old friends — the wild blades, when he gallivanted the land.

For that proud, wayward man now my heart breaks —
Breaks for that man whose mind was a secret eyrie,
Whose kind hand was sole signet of his race,
Who curbed me, scorned my green ways, yet increasingly loved me
Till Death drew its grey blind down his face.

And yet I am pleased that even my reckless ways
Are living shades of his rich calms and passions —
Witnesses for him and for those faint namesakes
With whom now he is one, under yew branches,
Yes, one in a graven silence no bird breaks.

For Rita with Love

You came home from school
on a special bus
full of people
who look like you
and love like you
and you met me
for the first time
and you loved me.
You love everybody
so much that it's not safe
to let you out alone.
Eleven years of love
and trust and time for you to learn
that you can't go on loving like this.
Unless you are stopped
you will embrace every person you see.
Normal people don't do that.
Some normal people will hurt you
very badly because you do.

Cripples don't look nice
but you embrace them.
You kissed a wino on the bus
and he broke down and he cried
and he said "Nobody has kissed me
for the last 30 years."
But you did.
You touched my face
with your fingers and said
"I like you."
The world will never
Be ready for you.
Your way is right
and the world will
never be ready.

We could learn everything
that we need to know
by watching you
going to your special school
in your special bus
full of people
who look like you
and love like you
and it's not safe
to let you out alone.
If you're not normal
there is very little hope
for the rest of us.

Pegasus

My soul was an old horse
Offered for sale in twenty fairs.
I offered him to the Church — the buyers
Were little men who feared his unusual airs.
One said: 'Let him remain unbid
In the wind and rain and hunger
Of sin and we will get him —
With the winkers thrown in—for nothing.'

Then the men of State looked at
What I'd brought for sale.
One minister, wondering if
Another horse-body would fit the tail
That he'd kept for sentiment —
The relic of his own soul —
Said, 'I will graze him in lieu of his labour.'
I lent him for a week or more
And he came back a hurdle of bones,
Starved, overworked, in despair.
I nursed him on the roadside grass
To shape him for another fair.

I lowered my price. I stood him where
The broken-winded, spavined stand
And crooked shopkeepers said that he
Might do a season on the land —
But not for high-paid work in towns.
He'd do a tinker, possibly.
I begged, 'O make some offer now,
A soul is a poor man's tragedy.
He'll draw your dungiest cart,' I said,
'Show you short cuts to Mass,
Teach weather lore, at night collect
Bad debts from poor men's grass.'
And they would not.

Where the
Tinkers quarrel I went down
With my horse, my soul.
I cried, 'Who will bid me half a crown?'
From their rowdy bargaining
Not one turned. 'Soul,' I prayed,
'I have hawked you through the world
Of Church and State and meanest trade.
But this evening, halter off,
Never again will it go on.
On the south side of ditches
There is grazing of the sun.
No more haggling with the world. . . .'

As I said these words he grew
Wings upon his back. Now I may ride him
Every land my imagination knew.

An Bonnán Buí

A bhonnáin bhuí, is é mo chrá do luí
is do chnámha críon tar éis a gcreim,
is chan díobháil bídh ach easpa dí
d'fhág tú 'do luí ar chúl do chinn;
is measa liom féin ná scrios na Traí
thú bheith sínte ar leacaibh lom,
is nach ndearna tú díth ná dolaidh
is tír is nárbh fhearr leat fíon ná uisce poill.

Is a bhonnáin álainn, mo mhíle crá
do chúl ar lár amuigh insa tslí,
is gur moch gach lá a chluininn do ghráig
ar an láib agus tú ag ól na dí;
is é an ní adeir cách le do dhearthháir Cathal
go bhfaighidh mé bás mar súd, más fíor;
ní hamhlaidh atá — súd an préachán breá
chuaigh a dh'éag ar ball, gan aon bhraon dí.

A bhonnáin óig, is é mo mhíle brón
thú bheith romham i measc na dtom,
is na lucha móra ag triall chun do thórraimh
ag déanamh spóirt is pléisiúir ann;
dá gcuirfeá scéala in am fá mo dhéinse
go raibh tú i ngéibheann nó i mbroid fá dheoch,
do bhrisfinn béim ar an loch sin Vesey
a fhliuchfadh do bhéal is do chorp isteach.

Ní hé bhur n-éanlaith atá mise ag éagnach,
an lon, an smaolach, ná an chorr ghlas —
ach mo bhonnán buí a bhí lán den chroí,
is gur cosúil liom féin é ina ghné is a dhath;
bhíodh sé choíche ag síoról na dí,
agus deir na daoine go mbím mar sin seal,
is níl deor dá bhfaighead nach ligfead síos
ar eagla go bhfaighinnse bás den tart.

Dúirt mo stór liom ligean den ól
nó nach mbeinnse beo ach seal beag gearr,

ach dúirt mé léi go dtug sí bréag
is gurbh fhaide mo shaolsa an deoch úd a fháil
nach bhfaca sibh éan an phíobáin réidh
a chuaigh a dh'éag den tart ar ball? —
a chomharsain chléibh, fliuchaidh bhur mbéal,
óir chan fhaigheann sibh braon i ndiaidh bhur mbáis.

Tranlation Thomas Kinsella page 147.

The Last Rose of Summer

'Tis the last rose of summer
Left blooming alone;
All her lovely companions
Are faded and gone;
No flower of her kindred,
No rose-bud is nigh,
To reflect back her blushes,
Or give sigh for sigh.

I'll not leave thee, thou lone one!
To pine on the stem;
Since the lovely are sleeping,
Go, sleep thou with them.
Thus kindly I scatter
Thy leaves o'er the bed,
Where thy mates of the garden
Lie scentless and dead.

So soon may I follow,
When friendships decay,
And from Love's shining circle
The gems drop away.
When true hearts lie wither'd,
And fond ones are flown,
Oh! who would inhabit
This bleak world alone?

An tEarrach Thiar

Fear ag glanadh cré
De ghimseán spáide
Sa gciúnas séimh
I mbrothall lae:
    Binn an fhuaim
    San Earrach thiar.

Fear ag caitheamh
Cliabh dá dhroim,
Is an fheamainn dhearg
Ag lonrú
I dtaitneamh gréine
Ar dhuirling bhán:
    Niamhrach an radharc
    San Earrach thiar.

Mná i locháin
In íochtar díthrá,
A gcótaí craptha,
Scáilí thíos fúthu:
    Támhradharc sítheach
    San Earrach thiar.

Tollbhuillí fanna
Ag maidí rámha,
Currach lán éisc
Ag teacht chun cladaigh
Ar órmhuir mhall
In ndeireadh lae:
    San Earrach thiar.

Oíche Nollaig na mBan

Bhí fuinneamh sa stoirm a éalaigh aréir,
    Aréir oíche Nollaig na mBan,
As gealt-teach iargúlta tá laistiar den ré
    Is do scréach tríd an spéir chughainn 'na gealt,
Gur ghíosc geataí comharsan mar ghogallach gé,
Gur bhúir abhainn shlaghdánach mar tharbh,
Gur múchadh mo choinneal mar bhuille ar mo bhéal
    A las 'na splanc obann an fhearg.

Ba mhaith liom go dtiocfadh an stoirm sin féin
    An oíche go mbeadsa go lag
Ag filleadh abhaile ó rince an tsaoil
    Is solas an pheaca ag dul as,
Go líonfaí gach neomat le liúirigh ón spéir,
    Go ndéanfaí den domhan scuaine scread,
Is ná cloisfinn an ciúineas ag gluaiseascht fám dhéin,
    Ná inneall an ghluaisteáir

MISE ÉIRE

Mise Éire
Sine mé ioná an Chailleach Béarra.

Mór mo ghlóir
Mé do rug Cú Chulainn cródha.

Mór mo náir
Mo chlann féin do dhíol a máthair.

Mise Éire
Uaignighe mé ioná an Chailleach Béarra.

Poet's own translation page 149.

THE HOST OF THE AIR

O'Driscoll drove with a song
The wild duck and the drake
From the tall and the tufted reeds
Of the drear Hart Lake.

And he saw how the reeds grew dark
At the coming of night-tide,
And dreamed of the long dim hair
Of Bridget his bride.

He heard while he sang and dreamed
A piper piping away,
And never was piping so sad,
And never was piping so gay.

And he saw young men and young girls
Who danced on a level place,
And Bridget his bride among them,
With a sad and a gay face.

The dancers crowded about him
And many a sweet thing said,
And a young man brought him red wine
And a young girl white bread.

But Bridget drew him by the sleeve
Away from the merry bands,
To old men playing at cards
With a twinkling of ancient hands.

The bread and the wine had a doom,
For these were the host of the air;
He sat and played in a dream
Of her long dim hair.

He played with the merry old men
And thought not of evil chance,
Until one bore Bridget his bride
Away from the merry dance.

He bore her away in his arms,
The handsomest young man there,
And his neck and his breast and his arms
Were drowned in her long dim hair.

O'Driscoll scattered the cards
And out of his dream awoke:
Old men and young men and young girls
Were gone like a drifting smoke;

But he heard high up in the air
A piper piping away,
And never was piping so sad,
And never was piping so gay.

Leda and the Swan

A sudden blow: the great wings beating still
Above the staggering girl, her thighs caressed
By the dark webs, her nape caught in his bill,
He holds her helpless breast upon his breast.

How can those terrified vague fingers push
The feathered glory from her loosening thighs?
And how can body, laid in that white rush,
But feel the strange heart beating where it lies?

A shudder in the loins engenders there
The broken wall, the burning roof and tower
And Agamemnon dead.
Being so caught up,
So mastered by the brute blood of the air,
Did she put on his knowledge with his power
Before the indifferent beak could let her drop?

A Prayer for my Daughter

Once more the storm is howling, and half hid
Under this cradle-hood and coverlid
My child sleeps on.
There is no obstacle
But Gregory's wood and one bare hill
Whereby the haystack — and roof-levelling wind,
Bred on the Atlantic, can be stayed;
And for an hour I have walked and prayed
Because of the great gloom that is in my mind.

I have walked and prayed for this young child an hour
And heard the sea-wind scream upon the tower,
And under the arches of the bridge, and scream
In the elms above the flooded stream;
Imagining in excited reverie
That the future years had come,
Dancing to a frenzied drum,
Out of the murderous innocence of the sea.

May she be granted beauty and yet not
Beauty to make a stranger's eye distraught,
Or hers before a looking-glass, for such,
Being made beautiful overmuch,
Consider beauty a sufficient end,
Lose natural kindness and maybe
The heart-revealing intimacy
That chooses right, and never find a friend.

Helen being chosen found life flat and dull
And later had much trouble from a fool,
While that great Queen, that rose out of the spray,
Being fatherless could have her way
Yet chose a bandy-legged smith for man.
It's certain that fine women eat
A crazy salad with their meat
Whereby the Horn of Plenty is undone.

In courtesy I'd have her chiefly learned;
Hearts are not had as a gift but hearts are earned
By those that are not entirely beautiful;
Yet many, that have played the fool
For beauty's very self, has charm made wise,
And many a poor man that has roved,
Loved and thought himself beloved,
From a glad kindness cannot take his eyes.

May she become a flourishing hidden tree
That all her thoughts may like the linnet be,
And have no business but dispensing round
Their magnanimities of sound,
Nor but in merriment begin a chase,
Nor but in merriment a quarrel.
O may she live like some green laurel
Rooted in one dear perpetual place.

My mind, because the minds that I have loved,
The sort of beauty that I have approved,
Prosper but little, has dried up of late,
Yet knows that to be choked with hate
May well be of all evil chances chief.
If there's no hatred in a mind
Assault and battery of the wind
Can never tear the linnet from the leaf.

An intellectual hatred is the worst,
So let her think opinions are accursed.
Have I not seen the loveliest woman born
Out of the mouth of Plenty's horn,
Because of her opinionated mind
Barter that horn and every good
By quiet natures understood
For an old bellows full of angry wind?

Considering that, all hatred driven hence,
The soul recovers radical innocence
And learns at last that it is self-delighting,
Self-appeasing, self-affrighting,

And that its own sweet will is Heaven's will;
She can, though every face should scowl
And every windy quarter howl
Or every bellows burst, be happy still.

And may her bridegroom bring her to a house
Where all's accustomed, ceremonious;
For arrogance and hatred are the wares
Peddled in the thoroughfares.
How but in custom and in ceremony
Are innocence and beauty born?
Ceremony's a name for the rich horn,
And custom for the spreading laurel tree.

June 1919.

All Lengendary Obstacles

All legendary obstacles lay between
Us, the long imaginary plain,
The monstrous ruck of mountains
And, swinging across the night,
Flooding the Sacramento, San Joaquin,
The hissing drift of winter rain.

All day I waited, shifting
Nervously from station to bar
As I saw another train sail
By, the San Francisco Chief or
Golden Gate, water dripping
From great flanged wheels.

At midnight you came, pale
above the negro porter's lamp.
I was too blind with rain
And doubt to speak, but
Reached from the platform
Until our chilled hands met.

You had been travelling for days
With an old lady, who marked
A neat circle on the glass
With her glove, to watch us
Move into the wet darkness
Kissing, still unable to speak.

from THE LAMENT FOR ART Ó LAOGHAIRE

The extracts in this section appear to have been uttered by Eibhlín over her husband's body in Carriginima.

Translation THOMAS KINSELLA

My steadfast love!
When I saw you one day
by the market-house gable
my eye gave a look
my heart shone out
I fled with you far
from friends and home.

And never was sorry:
you had parlours painted
rooms decked out
the oven reddened
and loaves made up
roasts on spits
and cattle slaughtered;
I slept in a duck-down
till noontime came
or later if I liked.

My steadfast friend!
It comes to my mind
that fine Spring day
how well your hat looked
with the drawn gold band,
the sword silver-hilted,
your fine brave hand
and menacing prance,
and the fearful tremble
of treacherous enemies.
You were set to ride
your slim white-faced steed
and Saxons saluted
down to the ground,

not from good will
but by dint of fear
— though you died at their hands,
my soul's beloved . . . .

My steadfast friend!
I didn't credit your death
till your horse came home
and her reins on the ground,
your heart's blood on her back
to the polished saddle
where you sat — where you stood. . . .
I gave a leap to the door,
a second leap to the gate
and a third on your horse. . . .

The Poet Raftery

Translation CRIOSTÓIR Ó FLOINN

I'm the Poet Raftery,
A man of hope and love,
There's no light in these eyes,
My peace is undisturbed.

As I wander on my way
By my heart's light I go,
I'm worn out and weary
At the end of each road.

Consider me now
With my face to the wall,
Playing music for pockets
That hold nothing at all.

THE MIDNIGHT COURT
Translation DAVID MARCUS

'O Aeval, greetings from my heart
To you, who Craglee's ruler art;
Our sun by day, our moon by night,
Our only comfort and delight,
O strong protector, firm and true,
Munster and Ireland depend on you;
The start of my story, the source of my strain,
The reason I'm senseless and almost insane,
The thing that has taken and torn me in twain
And has pricked me with pangs and has plagued me with pain—
Is the number of women, old and young,
For whom no wedding-bells have rung,
Who become in time mere hags and crones
Without man or money to warm their bones.
Thousands will back my evidence,
And I speak, alas, from experience;
Like me, I can swear, there's many another
Aching to be a wife and mother,
But the way we're ignored you'd think we're wrecks
Possessed of gender but not of sex;
At night with longing I'm lacerated,
Alone in bed I lie frustrated
And damned with dreams of desire denied
My hunger goes unsatisfied.
O Aeval, you must find a way
To save our women without delay,
For if the men are allowed to shirk
We'll have to force them to do their work.
By the time they're ready to take a wife
They're not worth taking to save their life,
They're stiff and shrunken and worn and weak
And when they mount you they wheeze and creak.
Then if, by chance, some lusty beau
Whose beard has hardly begun to grow
Decides to marry, whom does he wed—
Not a girl who is finely-bred,
With fawn-like figure and fetching face,
Who knows how to carry herself with grace,
But a wicked witch or a female scrooge
Who gathered her dowry by subterfuge! . . .'

Cill Chais

Translation THOMAS KINSELLA

Now what will we do for timber,
with the last of the woods laid low?
There's no talk of Cill Chais or its household
and its bell will be struck no more.
That dwelling where lived the good lady
most honoured and joyous of women
— earls made their way over wave there
and the sweet Mass once was said.

Ducks' voices nor geese do I here there,
nor the eagle's cry over the bay,
nor even the bees at their labour
bringing honey and wax to us all.
No birdsong there, sweet and delightful,
as we watch the sun go down,
nor cuckoo on top of the branches
settling the world to rest.

A mist on the boughs is descending
neither daylight nor sun can clear.
A stain from the sky is descending
and the waters receding away.
No hazel nor holly nor berry
but boulders and bare stone heaps,
not a branch in our neighbourly haggard,
and the game all scattered and gone.

Then a climax to all of our misery:
the prince of the Gael is abroad
oversea with that maiden of mildness
who found honour in France and Spain.

Her company now must lament her,
who would give yellow money and white
— she who'd never take land from the people
but was friend to the truly poor.

I call upon Mary and Jesus
to send her safe home again:
dances we'll have in long circles
and bone-fires and violin music;
that Cill Chais, the townland of our fathers,
will rise handsome on high once more
and till doom — or the Deluge returns —
we'll see it no more laid low.

County Mayo
Translation CRIOSTÓIR Ó FLOINN

Now with the springtime the day will be stretching,
When Bríd's day has gone by then I'll run up my sail,
Since this notion I've taken I'll never be resting
Till to County Mayo I have made my safe way.
Claremorris the first night is where I'll be nesting,
And not far off in Balla my first drink I'll take,
To Kiltimagh then, there a month I'll be spending,
From Ballinamore just two miles away.

I solemnly swear that my heart fills with joy
Like the wind rising up and the fog far off blown,
When my thoughts turn to Carra or to Gallen close by,
To Sgahaghaveela and the plains of Mayo.
Killeadin is the place where all fruits you can find,
Blackberries, raspberries, there everything grows,
And if I could be standing among my own kind
The years would drop off, I'd be youthful once more.

A Woman of the Mountain Keens her Son

Poet's own translation

Grief on the death, it has blackened my heart:
It has snatched my love and left me desolate,
Without friend or companion under the roof of my house,
But this sorrow in the midst of me, and I keening.

As I walked the mountain in the evening
The birds spoke to me sorrowfully,
The sweet snipe spoke and the voiceful curlew
Relating to me that my darling was dead.

I called to you and your voice I heard not,
I called again and I got no answer,
I kissed your mouth, and O God how cold it was!
Ah, cold is your bed in the lonely churchyard.

O green-sodded grave in which my child is,
Little narrow grave, since you are his bed,
My blessing on you, and thousands of blessings
On the green sods that are over my treasure.

Grief on the death, it cannot be denied,
It lays low, green and withered together,—
And O gentle little son, what tortures me is
That your fair body should be making clay!

The Ship

Translation THEO DORGAN

A ship came in from Valparaiso,
Let go her anchor in the bay,
Her name flashed bright, it brought to mind
A land of plenty, of sun and fame.

"Come," she said, "on a long journey
Away from this land of cloud and mist;
Under the Andes blue-grey slopes
There's a jewel-city, by the sun kissed."

But I was young and would not go,
My life before me, full of hope;
I still believed there lay before me
All the wonder of story and poem.

She hoisted sail, put out to sea,
Long long ago, her mast like gold,
Wrote her story on night's parchment
High where the stars shine bright and cold.

And still I know she will return,
I'll see the white city beneath the slopes
On the quiet shore of the Sea of Peace —
I still believe, dear God, still hope.

The Yellow Bittern
Translation THOMAS KINSELLA

Bittern, I'm sorry to see you stretched
with your bones decayed and eaten away.
Not want of food but need of a drink
has brought you so to lie face up.
I feel it worse than the ruin of Troy
to see you stretched on the naked stones,
who caused no hurt nor harm in the world,
as happy with boghole water as wine.

It hurts, fair bittern, a thousandfold
— your fallen head on the open road,
whose honk I heard in the early mornings
out on the mud as you took your drink.
Everyone tells your brother Cathal
that's certainly how I'm going to die.
Not so. Behold this handsome bird
lately dead for want of a drop.

Sorrow, young bittern, a thousandfold
to see you before me among the clumps,
and the big rats travelling toward your wake,
taking part in the fun and games.
If only you'd sent me word in time
that you were in trouble and needed a drink
I'd have dealt a blow at Vesey's lake
would have wetted your mouth and your innards too.

Your other birds I don't lament,
blackbird, thrush, or the grey crane,
but my yellow bittern full of heart
so like myself in face and hue.
He was for ever taking a drink
and they say I'm the same from time to time
— but I'll leave undrunk no drop I find
for fear I'd catch my death of thirst.

My darling said give up the drink
or I've only a little while to live
but I told her that she told a lie,
the selfsame drink prolongs my life.
Have ye not seen this smooth-necked bird
that died of thirst a while ago?
Wet your lips, my neighbours dear.
There won't be a drop when you're dead and gone.

I AM IRELAND
Poet's own translation

I am Ireland:
I am older than the Old Woman of Beare.

Great my glory:
I that bore Cuchulainn the valiant.

Great my shame:
My own children that sold their mother.

I am Ireland:
I am lonelier than the Old Woman of Beare.

Index of First Lines

INDEX OF POETS & TRANSLATIONS

ACKNOWLEDGEMENTS

The publishers sincerely thank the following:

Colm Tóibín for the moving Introduction.
Caroline Walsh Literary Editor of *The Irish Times* and Theo Dorgan, Director of Poetry Ireland/Éigse Éireann for writing the Foreword.
Gerry Smyth, *Irish Times* Managing Editor for his pragmatic outlook and advice.
Joan Ardiff of Mahon's Printers without whose assistance this publication would not be possible. Deirdre Davitt Foras na Gaeilge for her assistance with the poems in Irish.

Special thanks are due to Poetry Ireland/Éigse Éireann, whose Director Theo Dorgan acted as mentor to this publication; to all the staff, in particular Claire Doyle, Joe Woods and Paul Lenehan for their ready assistance in tracing valuable source material; also to Niamh Morris who was with the staff at the start of this project.

PERMISSIONS

Permission to use copyright material is gratefully acknowledged to the following:

Eavan Boland for 'Night Feed' from *Night Feed* (1982). R. Dardis Clarke, 21 Pleasants Street, Dublin 8, for 'The Planters' Daughter', 'The Lost Heifer' by Austin Clarke from *The Oxford Book of Irish Verse* (1958) and 'The Blackbird of Derrycairn' from *The Faber Book of Irish Verse* (1974). Máire Colum O'Sullivan for 'An Old Woman of the Roads', 'She Moved Through the Fair', 'A Cradle Song', 'A Drover' by Padraic Colum from *The Collected Poems Padraic Colum 1932–1953* (1953). Cló Iar- Chonnachta Teo. for 'Mise Raifteirí' and 'Contae Mhaigh Eo'. Máire Cruise O'Brien for 'An Long' by her uncle Pádraig de Brun (1975). Patrick Deeley for the extract from 'Woodman' taken from *Names for Love* (1990). Paul Durcan for 'Going Home to Mayo' from *The Penguin Book of Contemporary Irish Poetry* (1990) and for the extract from *Christmas Day* (1996). The Gallery Press for 'Death of an Irishwoman' by Michael Hartnett taken from *Selected and New Poems* (1994). Faber & Faber for the extracts from 'Clearances' and 'Station Island'; and for 'Mid-Term Break', 'Digging', 'Personal Helicon', 'Blackberry-Picking', 'Death of a Naturalist', 'Requiem for the Croppies', 'Follower', 'Postscript' by Seamus Heaney from *Opened Ground: Poems 1966-*

1996 (1998). Ruth Dodd for 'Padraig Ó Conaire, Gaelic Storyteller' and 'Father and Son' by her uncle F.R. Higgins from *The Oxfrod Book of Irish Verse* (1958). Pat Ingoldsby for 'For Rita With Love' from *Half a Hug* Collection, Willow Publications (1998). The Trustees of the Estate of the late Katherine B. Kavanagh, through the Jonathan Williams Literary Agency for the extracts from 'The Great Hunger'; and for 'On Raglan Road', 'Canal Bank Walk', 'Stony Grey Soil', 'In Memory of my Mother', 'A Christmas Childhood', 'Advent', 'Iniskeen Road, July Evening', 'Lines Written on a Seat on the Grand Canal, Dublin 'Erected to the Memory of Mrs Dermot O'Brien', 'Epic', 'Spraying the Potatoes', 'Pegasus'. Reprinted from *Patrick Kavanagh, Selected Poems, edited by Antoinette Quinn* (Penguin Books, 1996). Thomas Kinsella for 'Another September', 'Mirror in February' from *Poems 1956 – 1973 by Thomas Kinsella* (1980). The Gallery Press and the author for 'All Legendary Obstacles' by John Montague from *Collected Poems* (1995). David Higham Associates for the extract from 'Autumn Journal'; and for 'Snow' and 'Dublin' by Louis MacNeice taken from *Collected Poems* Faber & Faber (1996). Faber & Faber for the extract from 'Incantata' taken from 'The Annals of Chile' by Paul Muldoon from *New Selected Poems 1968-1994* (1996). The O'Nolan Estate for 'A Pint of Plain is your only Man' (The Workman's Friend) by Flann O'Brien from *At Swim-Two-Birds* (1960). Sáirséal Ó Marcaigh for 'Cúl an Tí' and 'Oíche Nollaig na mBan' by Seán Ó Ríordáin and 'An tEarrach Thiar' by Máirtín Ó'Direáin. The Estate of Katharine Tynan for 'Sheep and Lambs' from *The Oxford Book of Irish Verse* (1958). A.P. Watt Ltd. on behalf of Michael B. Yeats for extracts from 'The Tower'; and for 'The Lake Isle of Innisfree', 'He Wishes for the Cloths of Heaven', 'The Song of the Wandering Aengus', 'Easter, 1916', 'When You are Old', 'The Stolen Child', 'Sailing to Byzantium', 'The Wild Swans at Coole', 'September 1913', 'Among Schoolchildren', 'The Second Coming', 'An Irish Airman Foresees his Death', 'The Fiddler of Dooney', 'The Circus Animals' Desertion', 'The Fisherman', 'To a Child Dancing in the Wind', 'The Ballad of Father Gilligan', 'Red Hanrahan's Song about Ireland', 'Broken Dreams', 'Down by the Salley Gardens', 'Under Ben Bulben', 'The Host of the Air', 'Leda and the Swan', 'A Prayer for my Daughter' by W.B. Yeats taken from *The Collected Poems of W.B. Yeats.*

THE 100 MOST NOMINATED IRISH POEMS

1. *The Lake Isle of Innisfree,* W.B. Yeats

2. *He Wishes for the Cloths of Heaven,* W.B. Yeats

3. *Mid-Term Break,* Seamus Heaney

4. *The Song of Wandering Aengus,* W.B. Yeats

5. *On Raglan Road,* Patrick Kavanagh

6. *Easter, 1916,* W.B. Yeats

7. *When You are Old,* W.B. Yeats

8. *Canal Bank Walk,* Patrick Kavanagh

9. *Stony Grey Soil,* Patrick Kavanagh

10. *The Stolen Child,* W.B. Yeats

11. *An Old Woman of the Roads,* Padraic Colum
11. *In Memory of my Mother,* Patrick Kavanagh
11. *Sailing to Byzantium,* W.B. Yeats
11. *The Wild Swans at Coole,* W.B. Yeats

15. *The Deserted Village,* Oliver Goldsmith

16. T*he Ballad of Reading Gaol,* Oscar Wilde
16. *September, 1913,* W.B.Yeats

18. *Digging,* Seamus Heaney
18. *A Christmas Childhood,* Patrick Kavanagh
18. *The Wayfarer,* P.H. Pearse

21. *Advent,* Patrick Kavanagh
21. *I See His Blood upon the Rose,* Joseph Mary Plunkett

23. *The Great Hunger,* Patrick Kavanagh

24. *Thomas McDonagh,* Francis Ledwidge
24. *The Mother,* P.H. Pearse

26. *The Planter's Daughter,* Austin Clarke
26. *Caoineadh Áirt Uí Laoghaire,* Eibhlín Dubh Ní Chonaill
26. *Among Schoolchildren,* W.B. Yeats
26. *The Second Coming,* W.B. Yeats

30. *Iniskeen Road, July Evening,* Patrick Kavanagah

31. *Lines Written on a Seat on the Grand Canal, Dublin, 'Erected to the Memory of Mrs Dermot O'Brien',* Patrick Kavanagh
31. *An Irish Airman Foresees his Death,* W.B. Yeats

33. *Clearances,* Seamus Heaney
33. *Epic,* Patrick Kavanagh
33. *Another September,* Thomas Kinsella

36. *The Lost Heifer,* Austin Clarke
37. *A Disused Shed in Co. Wexford,* Derek Mahon

38. *June,* Francis Ledwidge
38. *Snow,* Louis MacNeice

40. *Personal Helicon,* Seamus Heaney
40. *Mise Raifteirí,* Antoine Ó Raifteirí

42. *Mirror in February,* Thomas Kinsella
42. *Cúirt an Mheán Oíche,* Brian Merriman
42. *Cill Chais,* Aodhagán Ó Rathaille
42. *The Fiddler of Dooney,* W.B. Yeats

46. *The Blackbird of Derrycairn,* Austin Clarke
46. *Blackberry-Picking,* Seamus Heaney
46. *Spraying the Potatoes,* Patrick Kavanagh
46. *The 'Workman's Friend', A Pint of Plain is Your Only Man,* Flann O'Brien
46. *Co. Maigheo (Anois Teacht an Earraigh),* Antoine Ó Raifteirí
46. *The Circus Animals' Desertion,* W.B. Yeats
46. *The Fisherman,* W.B. Yeats

53. *Ecce Puer,* James Joyce
53. *Incantata,* Paul Muldoon
53. *Cúl an Tí,* Seán Ó Riordáin
53. *To a Child Dancing in the Wind,* W.B. Yeats
53. *The Tower,* W.B.Yeats

58. *Night Feed,* Eavan Boland
58. *She Moved Through the Fair,* Padraic Colum
58. *Death of a Naturalist,* Seamus Heaney
58. *Requiem for the Croppies,* Seamus Heaney
58. *Autumn Journal,* Louis MacNeice
58. *Dublin,* Louis MacNeice
58. *Dark Rosaleen,* James Clarence Mangan
58. *The Meeting of the Waters,* Thomas Moore
58. *Bean tSléibhe ag Caoineadh a Mic,* Pádraig Mac Piarais
58. *The Ballad of Father Gilligan,* W.B. Yeats
58. *Red Hanrahan's Song about Ireland,* W.B. Yeats

69. *The Fairies,* William Allingham
69. *Pangur Bán,* Anon.
69. *Follower,* Seamus Heaney
69. *Padraic Ó Conaire, Gaelic Storyteller,* F.R. Higgins
69. *To My Daughter Betty, The Gift of God,* Tom Kettle
69. *The Fool,* P.H. Pearse
69. *The Splendour of God,* Joseph Mary Plunkett
69. *Sheep and Lambs,* Katharine Tynan
69. *Broken Dreams,* W.B. Yeats
69. *Down by the Salley Gardens,* W.B. Yeats
69. *Under Ben Bulben,* W.B. Yeats

80. *An Long,* Monsignor Pádraig de Brún
80. *A Cradle Song,* Padraic Colum
80. *A Drover,* Padraic Colum
80. *Woodman,* Patrick Deeley
80. *Christmas Day,* Paul Durcan
80. *Going Home to Mayo,* Paul Durcan
80. *Death of an Irishwoman,* Michael Hartnett
80. *Postscript,* Seamus Heaney
80. *Station Island,* Seamus Heaney
80. *Father and Son,* F.R. Higgins
80. *For Rita with Love,* Pat Ingoldsby
80. *Pegasus,* Parick Kavanagh
80. *An Bonnán Buí,* Cathal Buí Mac Giolla Ghunna
80. *The Last Rose of Summer,* Thomas Moore
80. *An tEarrach Thiar,* Máirtín Ó Direáin

80. *Oíche Nollaig na mBan,* Seán Ó Ríordáin
80. *Mise Éire,* Pádraig Mac Piarais
80. *The Host of the Air,* W.B. Yeats
80. *Leda and the Swan,* W.B. Yeats
80. *A Prayer for my Daughter,* W.B. Yeats

100. *All Legendary Obstacles,* John Montague